OH M

Frank Muir

ONE GOOD TURN DESERVES ANOTHER
Old English Proverb

We now come to the sad bit. Misty-eyed with love, poor Starkers had not seen things too clearly. What he took to be a beautiful, bald lady otter drifting downstream into his arms was not an otter at all. It was not even a live animal.

A few days previously a band of hunters had made camp upstream, feasting and carousing as was their wont. At one point in their proceedings they found that the gourd in which they kept the wine had a tear in it and was leaking so they flung it into the river. Vaguely animal-shaped, and completely bald, it had drifted downstream . . .

The whole tragic occurrence was summed up in the following morning's newspaper headline:

Wine-Gourd, Torn, Deceives an Otter.

Also by Frank Muir and Denis Norden
in Methuen Paperbacks

THE MY WORD STORIES
TAKE MY WORD FOR IT

FRANK MUIR &
DENIS NORDEN

Oh, My Word

A fourth collection of stories from 'My Word!'
a panel game devised by
Edward J. Mason & Tony Shryane

METHUEN LONDON LTD

A Methuen Paperback

OH, MY WORD!
ISBN 0 413 50850 1

First published in Great Britain 1980
by Eyre Methuen Ltd

Copyright © 1980 by Frank Muir & Denis Norden

This edition published 1982
by Methuen London Ltd
11 New Fetter Lane, London EC4P 4EE

Printed and bound in Great Britain by
Cox & Wyman Ltd, Reading

Contents

Beware of Greeks bearing gifts

Virgil
'Aeneid'

WHO can you turn to when you've just spent six weeks in the throes of a living nightmare and now that it's over, your so-called nearest and dearest refuse to believe a word of it? Not that I want to give the impression that I'm angry about their strange reaction, because I'm not. Just terribly, terribly hurt.

Let me calm down and give you the background to my appalling ordeal. It began with nothing more sinister than a Dundee cake. I'd had the happy idea of presenting it, as a souvenir of Britain, to a young Californian lady who'd once acted as my secretary when I was working in Los Angeles and who was now enjoying a free two-week stay at a top Mayfair hotel as part of her prize for winning the Miss Nude America Contest. A contest she had only entered, as I tried to explain to the frozen faces that gathered round me when I gift-wrapped the cake, because her heart was set on becoming a librarian and she hoped the prize-money would finance her studies.

Conscious that I'd left behind an atmosphere which would have been considered unseasonable even in Greenland, I made my way to the Mayfair hotel and entered the lift. There were already a few people inside it, one of whom I immediately recognized. He was an Arab potentate I shall only refer to as Haroun Al Raschid, because his riches and power are such that were I even to hint at his real name it could precipitate an international crisis.

One of his entourage pressed the button and, as we proceeded upwards, I couldn't help noticing that Haroun was smiling at me. Well, I didn't say anything to acknow-ledge it because, after all, what kind of small-talk can one enter into with a strange Arab sheikh? ('Crept into any good tents lately?') But, to my surprise, it was he who add-ressed me. 'May I ask,' he said, 'are you Denis ben Norden, the wandering story-teller of the broadcasting car-avans?'

It was when I nodded modest assent that the reign of terror began. He made a sign to one of his bodyguards, a great bearded fellow who looked as if he could open parking-meters with his teeth. As a result, there was a movement behind me, something suddenly hit me on the back of my skull and everything went black.

When I woke up, it was with a headache that must have shown up on the Richter Scale. I was in one of the hotel's luxury suites – all splashing fountains and Maria Montez baroque – and I was lying on a pile of silken cushions, with the Arabs grouped round looking down at me with gloating fascination.

'What do you want of me?' I said, clutching my hands protectively round my Dundee Cake.

Immediately, a jewelled dagger was at my throat. 'One ill-advised move,' said the bearded man, 'and your Adam's apple will be on the other side of your neck.'

'I will tell you what you are here for,' said Haroun; and as he proceeded to do so I felt my knuckles whiten. Appa-rently, ever since the days of a bygone slave girl called Scheherazade, the ultimate status symbol among Arabian rulers has been to have your own live-in story-teller. A sort of human tranquillizer, to provide distraction when you get home exhausted from a heavy OPEC meeting. Haroun him-self had been scouring the world to find a suitable candid-ate for his own household, and he'd only come to London because an agent of his – a former Armenian fig-packer now working as a BBC Light Entertainment producer – had sent word about two chaps who performed exactly that function on an obscure radio panel-game.

I don't have to tell you, when I realized what he had in mind for me, my heart chilled. The prospect of spending the rest of my life doing a nightly turn for a desert despot . . .! Drawing a deep breath – 'I refuse,' I said resolutely.

In a flash, a gleaming scimitar was nudging me. 'How would you like to be turned into a soprano?' said the bearded man.

Faltering, I said, 'This should really have been arranged through my agent.'

'I will let you remain alive,' Haroun said, 'only as long as your stories amuse me.'

And so it proved. Every night for the next six weeks, the moment Haroun returned from a tough day putting up world petrol prices, he would seat himself expectantly before me and I'd launch into a typical *My Word!* story. Only when I saw that stern mouth relax could I feel reassured that, for another day at least, the pun had proved mightier than the sword.

It was an incarceration that might well have ended tragically had I not had the good fortune to attract the favour of one of the female members of Haroun's retinue. In deference to the world's need to conserve energy, he had only brought a small assortment of his wives with him – about a six-pack – but I soon noticed that one of them was eyeing me with what can only be described as a hungry look. Realizing that women have the same urges the world over, I promised that if she'd help me effect an escape, I'd oblige with what she so obviously had in mind: the Dundee cake. She proved as good as her word and I sped home.

As I've mentioned, the thing I still can't reconcile myself to is the attitude my dear ones have adopted towards the terrifying ordeal I have now related. What makes it especially trying is that they were the ones who kept *demanding* a reasonable explanation of how I could go off to a Miss Nude America's hotel and not come back for six whole weeks.

All I can now hope is that at least my experience will provide a moral for anyone else who makes his living from hastily improvised fiction. As that old Latin tag forewarned:

'Beware of sheikhs sharing lifts.'

The female of the species is more deadly
than the male

Rudyard Kipling
'The Female of the Species'

'Go, little book . . .' wrote Chaucer, drawing *Troilus and Criseyde* to its conclusion. Like a paper boat, the little volume was launched on the waters and wished well.

Robert Louis Stevenson sent *Envoy* on its way with a powerful suggestion that buying the book would radically improve the purchaser's lifestyle. He wrote:

> Go, little book,
> And wish to all,
> Flowers in the garden, meat in the hall,
> A bit of wine, a spice of wit,
> A house with lawns enclosing it,
> A living river by the door,
> A nightingale in the sycamore.

It seems that nowadays, in the fierce competition of the book world, sending a book on its way with a gentle prayer and a pat on the spine is about as efficient a method of distribution as hurling a boomerang. The method now in vogue is not to market the book at all but to market the author.

An author nowadays may still write, 'Go, little book . . .', but in all honesty he should add, '. . . but hang on, I am coming with you.'

My first Author Tour was a year or two ago but I still wake up at night shivering and twitching at the thought of it. I propose here and now to recount a few details of that trip so as to give a kind of Survival Guide to those of you proposing to burst into print.

My book was first published in the USA and my Author Tour started there. It was not so much a question of being sent out on circuit as being shot out of a cannon. I was given a pile of airline tickets, an itinerary, and away I went, unaccompanied, across the Middle West.

The first thing you have to get to grips with is the problem of taxis. In New York all taxis are yellow and dented. They are ex-saloon cars and most of the space formally given over to the passengers is taken up by a malefactor-proof steel grill. This means that anybody over four feet six inches in height – which I am – has to bend into a kind of foetal crouch on the back seat. While he can. The trouble is that New York cabbies are chatty. I had one whose greatest experience was once having driven the bandleader Geraldo. We careered across New York late at night singing – in harmony – 'You Stepped Out of a Dream'. The difficulty was that I had to get on my knees and talk to him through a small aperture in the steel grill. It was like travelling in a weird mobile confessional.

And then there was the problem of laundry on the tour. The itinerary called for one night only in every town so there was no question of handing the laundry in. I had to do it myself. For those of you who may have to face the same problem, here is my method.

N.B. American hotel washbasins do not have rubber plugs but those lever arrangements whereby you press a knob and the plug leaps out and when you pull it the plug leaps back into its hole. But the plug does not seat properly. *Ever*. So if you try to do your washing in the basin the suds disappear before you have got to the collar. But do not despair. Every American bathroom has a white waterproof wastepaper basket. Always use this.

On arriving in your hotel room at six thirty p.m. (it always is six thirty p.m. when you arrive; all American flights take fifty-five minutes, incidentally), ring Room Service and order a Club Sandwich. The girl will say, 'Right away, sir,' which will give you forty-five minutes to do your laundry before your supper arrives.

Strip off everything *except your socks* (for some reason to do with the shape of socks they cannot be washed in the hand). Shove your shirt, pants, hanky and whatever else you want to wash into the wastepaper basket, add detergent, hold it under the shower – on 'hot' – swill it round a bit and leave it. Take a shower – soaping your socks well *whilst still on your feet* – then dry yourself. Remove socks and hang on shower rail to dry.

Pound the garments in the wastepaper basket. Pour off the water and refill. Pound them again. Repeat until the water you pour away is reasonably transparent, then hang them on the shower rail to dry. *Except for the handkerchiefs.*

Dangle your hankies in water until they are sopping wet and then squeegee them with the edge of your hand on to the bathroom tiles. When you peel them off in the morning they will come away *ironed.*

The problems of an Author Tour in England, which came next, are different but just as grievous.

Trying to cram the ancient frame into a British Rail sleeping berth designed to accommodate nobody taller or wider than Beryl Bainbridge . . .

It was the night sleeper to Manchester, first class (the publishers insisted, rather as Torquemada always gave the subject of his Inquisition a rose). Sleeping compartments, I found, are not spacious but by sitting on the basin I could get my trousers off. I spent a happy hour playing with the little folding shelves and the lights and adjusting the paper drugget, and trying to work out what the piece of bent wire hanging from the door was for (I still do not know) and then I got into bed and tried to sleep. Sleep was not possible. The heating was on and would not turn off and the temperature was something like 140 degrees Fahrenheit. I stuffed a sock in the vent but the smell of hot sock soon became insupportable. I removed the charred sock, lay on top of the bedclothes and hoped for the best. Every time the train pulled up at a station, which it did eighteen times between London and Manchester, I fell off the bed.

Bone tired, shaken and bruised, I made a tour of Manchester bookshops and then presented myself at the . . . Hotel (name suppressed on legal advice) where I was to attend a Literary Luncheon.

It was the worst meal I have ever eaten.

It began with what it called 'Leak Soup'. This tasted like rusty water which had somehow leaked through the ceiling on to the plates.

The main course was supposed to be steak and kidney pie and vegetables. It had been hanging around for many hours and the steak and kidney pie tasted of Brussels sprouts, and the Brussels sprouts tasted of peas, and the peas had no taste at all.

Lastly there was apple pie. This was a kind of dim frog-spawn with a bit of cardboard on top.

The lunch was a truly deadly experience but worse was to come. The speeches. The first two were tolerable. A poet spoke briefly and quite inaudibly about a poet who died three hundred years ago of whom nobody had ever heard. He was followed by a large jolly man with a mottled face who wrote books about badgers and stoats and earwigs who talked like humans. He had clearly avoided the food and concentrated on knocking back the hock (which tasted like water that daffodils had stood in for a week). His speech was a string of racial jokes, some obscene but all offensive, which cheered us up a little.

Then came the star turn. A lady novelist. She read from a sheaf of notes the thickness of *Decline and Fall of the Roman Empire*, Vol. I, in a loud and hectoring voice which rattled the coffee cups. It also caused the microphone to go eeeeeeeeEEEE*EEEE*! which went through the head like an assegai. It was difficult to follow the drift of her argument as she dropped her notes through nerves after a minute and scooped them up again in the wrong order but it seemed to be a minute-by-minute description of her working day. As this consisted almost wholly of staring at a blank sheet of paper, chewing a biro and wallowing in self-pity, it did not make for merry listening. After thirty minutes half the guests were asleep. After forty-five minutes the other half had left. She finished, after fifty-eight minutes on her feet, to a patter of applause from the committee and two ladies who were staying in the hotel and had joined the lunch by mistake.

So I conclude my Author's Survival Guide with an apt quotation from Rudyard Kipling, who had suffered and knew what he was talking about.

Avoid Literary Lunches if possible. If they are anything like mine the food is awful. But that is not all:

The female of the speeches is more deadly than the meal.

You can lead a horse to water
but you cannot make him drink

Proverb

IT'S probably due to some kind of personality defect, but I just don't seem to have the knack of bribing people effectively. Perhaps I don't put out the correct feelers, perhaps I don't phrase the proposition properly, perhaps the inducements I dangle just aren't suitable – whatever the reason, I simply don't appear to be blessed with any kind of talent for corruption.

And that's a shame. Because where Frank and the editor of *The Guinness Book of Records* were concerned I really wanted to succeed. Strange about Frank, that. Did you know – and not many people know this – despite all the honours and tokens of public acclaim that have been showered upon Frank Muir, many of them from a great height, the one honour he most avidly craves still eludes him? I'm talking about seeing his name in *The Guinness Book of Records*.

No, I didn't believe it either when he first confessed it to me. But after I discovered it to be true, I found myself – well, I dunno – moved. Big tall fellow like that, all the poise in the world, pink bow tie, and yet going on deep down inside him, there's something quite different from what gnaws away at us ordinary folk. Nothing to do with Elsie Tanner or the second Nolan Sister or Olga Korbut. His most burning secret desire is to have his name recorded in that brewery book.

I don't mind telling you, that made such an impression on me that I went out and bought a copy. After a prolonged study of it, I came back and reported to Frank. 'Seems to me,' I said, 'that there's two ways most of 'em in there qualified for entry. Either by doing something nobody else had done before; or by doing something people had done before but doing it faster, longer or more often. Which of these alternatives appeals to you?'

'The first one,' he said unhesitatingly.

Do you know – and here's something else not many people know – it's awfully difficult to think of something nobody else has ever done before? I toyed with all sorts of possibilities; going over Niagara Falls on roller-skates; jogging nude round and round inside the Dorchester revolving-door; pushing an ice-cube across Richmond Common with your nose; being shot across Lake Windermere by a giant catapult suspended between two trees. All of them Frank rejected as either impossible, inconvenient or undignified. So we were forced to settle for the second alternative.

Leafing through the book, I came up with a couple of record-breakers Frank might try going one better than – 'Chap named Fyodor Vassilet of Moscow,' I said. 'He fathered sixty-nine children. Or Don Carter of Michigan who, by using quite different skills, balanced on one foot for eight hours forty-six minutes.'

In that pipe-smoking way of his, Frank pondered. 'How many children did you say that Russian fellow had?' he asked finally.

'Sixty-nine,' I said, 'but remember you start with the advantage of already having two. Cuts your target all the way down to sixty-eight.'

'True,' he said, and puffed away a bit more. Then – 'Trouble is,' he said, 'what I really had in mind was getting into next year's edition.'

'Lessens your chances,' I warned. 'Unless you're prepared to spread yourself round a bit.' He shook his head. I drew a line through Fyodor Vassilet's name and, after a moment's reflection, drew another through that of Don Carter. Knowing Frank as I do, I doubt whether he could balance for eight hours forty-six minutes even lying down.

Out came the book again and I searched for other feats of skill or endurance. The one that seemed to offer Frank the best opportunity of making the record book was that set up by a Mr Crosby of Harrogate, who earned his immortality by spitting a cherry-stone forty-two feet five and a half inches from a sitting position.

There and then I went out and bought two pounds of cooking cherries – well, it seemed needless extravagance to get the eating ones just for spitting purposes – and brought them to Frank. He settled himself in a comfortable arm-chair while I stood by with a tape measure.

As it turned out, long distance cherry-stone spitting is by no means as easy as it sounds. For one thing, it now appears that Frank shouldn't even have considered making his attempt on the spitting record from within the Savile Club. (Or so, at any rate, would seem to be the opinion of the current Membership Committee.) Secondly, it could be that this particular activity is not one that should be even attempted by anyone with a bridgework problem. (The number of times I had to dash out into Brook Street and retrieve it from under passing taxis!) Thirdly, did you know – and here's yet another thing not many people know – did you know there even *was* such an ailment as Dislocation of the Tongue?

Nevertheless, the moment the orthodontist had signed Frank off, there I was – Old Faithful – waiting with another record for him to better. This time, it was the one set up by Lindsay R. Dodd who walked backwards from Leeds, Yorkshire to Kendal, Cumberland.

Experience had taught us by now that before any record-breaking attempt, it was as well to estimate one's chances by having a practice go. So, after I'd worked a route out on the map, Frank set out from his home in Thorpe, Surrey, walking backwards in what I'd estimated would take him in a dead straight line to where I was waiting with a stop-watch in Marble Arch, London. It was only when he arrived eighteen hours late and wet from head to foot that I realized my map-reading had failed to take into account Staines Reservoir.

To give you all the details of what happened with the other records he set himself to break could well take a life-time, and as we obviously haven't got a lifetime let me simply enumerate some of them in such a way that it may seem like one. Among the record breakers my colleague went on to try to displace was Bob Blackmore who ate three lemons in twenty-four seconds – it took four of us three hours to get Frank's lips to unpucker; a man in Wolverhampton who jumped a twelve-foot billiard table lengthways – I *told* Frank to let go the cue; and Bill White, who was buried alive for 134 days. (It was after just fifteen seconds that we began hearing the muffled screams.)

'We'll have to try again with the first option,' I said finally. 'Doing something nobody has ever done before.'

'Like what?' said Frank.

'Like bribing the editor of *The Guinness Book of Records*,' I said. 'Leave it to me.'

Norris McWhirter has been editing the volumes since 1955 and whatever other faults he may have, he is at least approachable. When I invited him to a slap-up lunch at the Savoy Grill, he agreed readily. It was over the coffee that I made my move. 'See here, Mr McWhirter,' I said, 'I could make arrangements for you to eat this kind of meal regularly, providing you could bend a few rules to the extent of including in next year's edition the name of a man who has established what you could justify as a *sort* of record.'

He looked at me expressionlessly. 'What does "a sort of record" mean?'

'Well,' I said, 'isn't it in itself a record to have made more unsuccessful attempts to get into *The Guinness Book of Records* than anyone else on record?'

By way of answer, he picked up the jug of iced water, poured it carefully into my lap and left. See what I mean by my incompetence at bribery? Despite all the expensive food and drink I'd stuffed down that man, he refused to compromise his principles by one jot.

Perhaps I should have listened to the old proverb:

You can feed a Norris McWhirter but you cannot make him fink.

> It is a riddle wrapped in a mystery
> inside an enigma

Winston Churchill
Description of Russian foreign policy

KNOWING that my old friend Sherlock Holmes was partial to a newly-baked loaf, I stopped off at his bakers in Chamber Street before going on to his chambers in Baker Street.

But Holmes was not there.

This hardly surprised me. One day he might be in Marrakech removing secret papers from the safe of the Bosnian consulate in the guise of a Japanese wrestler, the next foiling an attempt to sabotage an assault on the Matterhorn in the guise of an Egyptian channel swimmer. There was no telling.

I settled myself in a comfortable old leather chair to await his return. The loaf looked delicious. I took a bite of the crust. It splintered with the noise of a small-calibre pistol shot and I was deluged with crumbs.

Quite a large part of my time was spent waiting for Holmes but this was no matter. I had no dependants to consider: I just sat there, a crusty old bachelor.

He, on the other hand, was the world's greatest criminologist; the ideal man to call upon when the Empire stood in jeopardy. I mused upon an idea I had had for some time of mounting an exhibition of relics of some of his greater triumphs: the odd hat-band, spy, dead dog and so forth. I would call it the Ideal Holmes Exhibition.

It was a quarter to five the following afternoon that I was interrupted from my reverie by a distant but unmistakable sound: the oath of a cabby who has been under-tipped. Moments later I heard footsteps on the stairs and Holmes appeared in the doorway. He flung his deerstalker hat away from him distractedly. It circled the room twice, clearly seeking a suitable landing site, before settling gently upon the beak of a stuffed ptarmigan. And then he saw me and his eyes lit up.

'Lily Langtry!' he cried, taking my hand. 'By all that's delightful!'

'It's me – Watson!' I said.

'Then what are you doing there in a dress covered with beige spots?' he demanded fiercely.

'They are breadcrumbs, old friend,' I said, brushing them off. I could see that he had something on his mind.

After a moment of restless pacing he suddenly said, 'I have just been given tea by Her Majesty's Foreign Secretary –'

'Earl Grey?'

'No,' he said. 'A fairly ordinary Darjeeling. Grown, I rather fancy, on that south-facing hill just above the hand-bag factory. He gave me very worrying news.'

Holmes paced the room again. The cat was sitting asleep on his chair and Holmes bent to tickle it behind an ear.

'Watson, my violin if you please.'

I handed it to him and with a forehand drive worthy of the great Dr Grace himself, he batted the cat out of the chair and on to the floor. He settled himself comfortably into the chair.

'I am informed, Watson, that there is in this country an important Balkan princeling, here under the protection of Her Britannic Majesty. He has travelled from his own squalid little country to Britain in order to undergo an operation at which our British surgeons lead the world. The removal of an in-growing toe-nail.'

'Just so. What we medical men call a "piggyectomy".'

'Would you mind shutting up while I'm talking?'

I nodded assent.

'The Foreign Office believe that an attempt is going to be made on the prince's life. Tonight.'

'But by whom? Holmes. By whom? – if you will pardon the understandable interruption.'

'There is a secret sect in Russia whose members are trained in all techniques of assassination. Their job is to spread out over Europe and foment revolution. They are fanatics and will stop at nothing – not even road signs saying "Major Road Ahead".'

'Good grief,' I whispered.

'When a member is fully trained there is a strange Russian indoctrination ceremony. Their leader, a mysterious lady known as Sister Anna, kisses him on both cheeks twice and he is then known by a special name.'

'What name?'

'He is thereafter known as an – Anarchist.'

My blood went cold.

'Our information is that they are in London and have their orders to poison the prince tonight, thus provoking a diplomatic incident which might lead to a major conflagration among the leading nations of Europe.'

Holmes had already taken every precaution. A police constable was on duty by the side of every bed in the Charing Cross Hospital where the prince lay. Eight men were on permanent duty round the prince's bed. No visitors were to be allowed in. The prince was to eat nothing and drink nothing until it was all over.

'Wait a minute, Holmes. The prince will be under an anaesthetic. Can they not get him *then* and make him swallow something?'

'He will not lose consciousness at any time. A local anaesthetic will be applied to his foot, which will go to sleep.'

'Ah yes. A condition we doctors call comatose.'

'What is worrying me, Watson, is that these fiends are masters of disguise. I am sure that they are already within the hospital disguised as porters, or matrons or bunches of grapes. But how – how, man – will they strike? How will they force the poison *down* him? They must force the poison *down* him in some manner or . . .' He paused, then continued softly, 'I've got it! I think I've got it! Why should we assume that they will attempt to force the poison *down* him? I must get to Charing Cross Hospital immediately, if not before . . .'

'But, Holmes, you have nothing to go on!'

'Then I will borrow your bike.'

I waited for two hours, fortifying myself with eating the remains of the loaf, which I found lodged within my waistcoat.

He strode into the room with a look of quiet triumph on his hawk-like face.

'The assassination will not take place,' he said. 'I found the murder device and the fiends have been apprehended, lurking within the hospital walls disguised as light diets. This is what they proposed to use to introduce the poison into the prince!'

He flung on to the table an object I knew well from my medical practice. It was a long rubber tube with a bulb at one end. Near the end of the tube was an odd bulge.

'There is the proof that the villains were Russian anarchists,' he cried.

'But how did they suppose to use this to poison the prince?' I faltered. 'By what system?'

'Alimentary, my dear Watson. If you will do me the goodness to take the device apart I will deduce what you will find therein.'

I did so.

'I think you will find,' said Holmes, 'that you have in your hand a wee doll, made of wood, with "Made in the Ukraine" stamped on its base.'

'Correct, Holmes.'

'It is, of course, the smallest of a nest of eight, which are popular with Russian children. Be careful how you handle it, Watson. Inside the doll will be a poison which is tasteless, odourless, colourless and for which even our music-halls have no known anecdote.'

'There seems to be a piece of paper wrapped around the doll, Holmes.'

'I think you will find that it is a page ripped at random from some cheap edition of a mystery novel. It is there to hold the doll firmly within the tube.'

'Correct. It is a page from Wilkie Collins's famous mystery, *The Woman in White*. Amazing, Holmes! But how did you deduce from this device that it spelled Russia?'

Holmes lit his pipe, injected himself with a snort of cocaine and played a swift chorus of Monti's *Czardas* on the violin before saying, quietly: 'See what it is, man–?

'It is a wee doll wrapped in a mystery inside an enema.'

Speak of one who loved not wisely, but too well

Shakespeare
'Othello'

BECAUSE the publication of the collected correspondence of the Duke of Wellington was one of the most talked-about literary events of the past few years, you can imagine my excitement when I recently came into possession of one of his unpublished letters. What's more, it is dated 1811, which means he wrote it before he was even made a duke; while, in fact, he was still plain Sir Arthur Wellesley. The postmark on the letter's envelope is Spain, it is addressed to his father's sister, a Miss H. Wellesley, and its content reads as follows:

Dear Auntie Hilda,

Thank you for the knitted things. We are presently encamped before Salamanca and the tent they have given me is very nice, if a bit on the small side, especially when I am on my horse. As you advised, I have taken the precaution, while encamped with the rough and licentious soldiery, to keep all my valuables in a safe place, even though this does tend to make me walk oddly.

But the purpose of this missive relates to something more important; namely, your constant urgings that I should find myself a nice girl for the purpose of getting married and perpetuating the Wellesley name. In that respect, I am moved to recount a strange occurrence which occurred soon after we made camp.

Late one evening, there came a knock at my tent-flap and when I bade whoever was without to make his way within, it turned out to be faithful Colour Sergeant Parker. When he spoke, I could not help but notice it was in a strangely hesitant tone, because his more customary method of reporting is at a pitch of voice to make your ears water. Accordingly – 'You seem to be labouring under the stress of some emotion, Colour Sergeant,' I remarked.

'Trouble in B Lines, sir,' he replied, one mutton-chop twitching noticeably.

Such tidings constitute no unusual occurrence among the sweepings I command. In fact, I can confide to you, dear Aunt – knowing that your discretion will never allow the comment to go further – that my troops may not frighten the enemy but, by G—, they frighten me. So I evinced no surprise, merely nodded him to proceed.

'I have reason to believe, sir,' he said, with even more difficulty, 'I have reason to believe that a certain fusilier in the fourth tent is – a female!'

Here, indeed, *was* an unusual occurrence. Need I say that the intelligence left me so put about, I removed the epaulettes from my pyjamas, replaced them upon my uniform and, bidding the Colour Sergeant bring the soldier hither immediately, redonned full military order. Within moments, what appeared to be a slim boyish fusilier was standing before me.

'At ease, soldier,' I said. 'Now what is this I hear? An accusation has been made that, contrary to Army Regulations, you have undertaken Active Service while knowingly being other than of the male gender. How do you answer this charge?'

By way of response, the young soldier removed his forage-cap and tossed his head. Then, dear Aunt, did I behold a sight that for one suffocating moment had me neglecting the inherent reflex of breathing. For, from the lad's shoulders, a cascade of golden hair shook itself loose and fell down behind him, descending to almost as far as where the back changes its name. At the spectacle, the Colour Sergeant gave such a sharp intake of breath, his side-whiskers were sucked down his throat and it became necessary for me to pound his shoulders to prevent him choking.

The fusilier was indeed a girl!

Endeavouring to regain my composure, I said to her,

'What can have induced you, a female, to join the colours?'

Her answer was immediate and confident, '"Twas, sir, for a pair of laughing brown eyes.'

Further interrogation elicited that the said eyes, brown, laughing, two, were the property of her betrothed, who had been pressed into service with the Limehouse Blues. 'And after he'd been taken away, sir,' she said, 'I found I couldn't do without him.'

'Couldn't do what without him?' I asked.

She coloured prettily. 'I joined the Army to find him and be at his side, sir.' Then she went on to explain the manner in which she had effected this difficult undertaking. Her first step had been to seek out a Recruiting Station with a near-sighted Medical Officer. Luck being with her, she was duly sworn in and posted to a regiment where, by reason of her boyish form and deepness of voice, she was able to maintain the deception for nearly twenty minutes.

The Colour Sergeant muttered an oath. 'So that's it,' he said. 'That's why B Troop have put in no applications for leave since 1809.'

But, suddenly aware that something within my heart was throbbing like a stubbed toe, I motioned him to silence. 'Tell me, child,' I said, 'What is your name?'

'Kitty,' she said. 'But they do call me Kit.'

Kit! My soul leaped. It was the name of my favourite inspection! Conscious of a certain dryness of throat, I pressed on. 'And the name of your betrothed? He of the laughing brown eyes?'

'If you please, sir,' she said. 'Fred Pacefoot.'

My lips tightened. Well did I remember Pacefoot – a slovenly, poltroonish malcontent. One of the few soldiers in the Peninsular to be demoted from Private to Semi-Private.

A sudden resolve stirred within me. Dismissing the Colour Sergeant, I addressed the girl urgently. 'Miss Kit,' I said. 'For some years now, my Auntie Hilda has been urging me to take a wife. Can I not now persuade you – moved as I am by the devoted gallantry you have exhibited – to forget this Pacefoot and think rather of exchanging your maiden name for that of Wellesley? For I can promise you much. Not only am I in prospect of being granted an Iron Dukedom, but there is every chance of having a popular boot named after me. What can a Fred Pacefoot offer to match that?'

Her answer was immediate. 'Sir – a pair of laughing brown eyes.' To which, dear Aunt, I had no answer but to allow her to leave my tent and continue her search.

Having already called upon your discretion once, I must seek it again. Because the initials of that girl will be carved forever on my ridge-pole, I must now ask you not to allow the tale I have told you about her to become the common tittle-tattle of your tea-time cronies.

Or if, perforce, you find yourself in some wise obliged to bandy about the story of that devoted girl, then do me this favour –

Speak of one who loved not Wellesley, but two eyes.

> There are fairies at the bottom of our garden
>
> *Rose Fyleman*
> *'Fairies'*

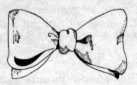

'**G**r-r-r – you swine!'

A bit strong, mayhap, for a literary work of this sensitivity? Not a bit of it. I merely quote Browning: *Soliloquy of the Spanish Cloister*.

When I am feeling as grim as I am now I frequently growl that line to people I meet. If they faint, or try to beat my skull in with a broken lump of concrete, I am able to recover my poise by murmuring, 'Don't you know your Browning?' They are then wrong-footed and usually apologize. Unless they are, at the time, sun-bathing.

What I am really suffering from is Progressive Melancholia brought on by the breakfast I had this morning. 'Progressive Melancholia' is an age-old malady which I have just invented. It is a good name because it works in both senses of the word 'progressive'. The melancholy gets progressively worse. And it is induced by what some misguided idiots – Gr-r-r – you swine – call progress.

Items we are supposed to regard as progress include:

(a) advertising a very good bar of chocolate not by the excellence of its ingredients, or its taste, or the nourishment it provides, but by the loudness of the noise it makes when you break it in half;

(b) printing telephone directories by computer so that the names are not *quite* in alphabetical order;

(c) putting up a notice which says 'For your convenience, all lifts are out of use for servicing';

(d) packing biscuits on airlines in such impenetrable

plastic envelopes that, wrench or bite as you may, you end up with a handful of biscuit-dust;

(e) replacing room service in hotels with an electric kettle whose lead is too short to reach the table so you have to grovel on your knees to mix together a plastic envelope containing too much sugar, a small plastic pot of something which is not milk but has curdled anyway, and a thin brown packet seemingly containing the ashes of a cremated mole.

Small grievances, you may think, amid the greater lunacies of our century. But I remind you that it is the tiny things, not the large, which irritate. A flea within the ear is unbearable. An elephant cannot get in.

My flea this morning was breakfast.

Do you remember breakfast? What happened to it?

Do you remember porridge? Hot goo which filled you up and made the ends of your fingers tingle?

For centuries porridge nourished the entire Scottish nation. Athletes trained on it and such was its energy-giving property that, during the Highland Games, cabers – entire pine-trees – were tossed high in the air as easily as if they were 2B lead pencils.

A good bath of porridge could grow hair on a haggis.

It was made on a Saturday night, poured into the kitchen drawer, and allowed to cool all Sunday while the family sat around repenting and refraining from whistling. At dawn on Monday the honest crofter would saw off a lump, stuff it into his sporran and set off up the hills for a week's sheep-gathering, confident that he would be well sustained by an occasional gnaw of the grey/beige oaten manna.

All gone now, with the arrival of progress. Porridge has now been improved and is what is known as 'instant porridge'. A food which is called 'instant' superficially resembles the original but has been dealt with chemically so that it takes slightly less time to prepare in return for losing ninety per cent of its flavour and all its nourishment.

Bacon is no longer bacon. It emerges, sweating heavily, from its plastic envelope and resists all efforts to fry it to crispness. The only hope is to continue frying for hours, hand on the gas tap. The slice of bacon will first shrivel, then shrink. At the very moment it is about to disappear,

27

entirely switch off the gas. The minute crumb of bacon you are left with will not be *crisp* – as we used to know and love crisp bacon – but it will be the best you can do these days.

And fried eggs. A fried egg should be sluttish. It should be irregular in shape and its petticoats should be frayed and none too clean.

In a hotel or a restaurant nowadays progress has decreed that fried eggs should be neat, clean and hygienic. The yolk is anaemic and the white is hospital white and slimy with oil. If you try to fork a piece when having breakfast in bed it slides off the fork and slithers down your chest, ending up in your tummy-button.

What we are given to eat for breakfast nowadays is called a 'cereal'. These products were invented by an American vegetarian called Post. He had the bright idea of providing vegetarians with an alternative to bacon and eggs. His method was to take an ear of corn, hit it with a smallish toffee-hammer until it was flat, then roast it in the oven and serve it with milk and sugar. As the world was going through one of its periodic fits of lunacy and deciding that anything new was better, these flakes of corn became hugely popular for breakfast. Other manufacturers got busy and hammered away at all sorts of other things like grains of rice and oats and wheat and bran. And they made them into all sorts of shapes so that they could claim them as 'new', i.e. better.

My wife has lately been breaking her fast with something called 'muesli'. It seems that some manufacturer decided that hitting a grain of cereal with a toffee-hammer was too painful on the finger and thumb of the left hand and there must be an easier way of earning a fortune. So he hit upon the simple notion of emptying out the leavings of cart-horses' nosebags, adding a few other things like un-consumed portions of chicken layers' mash and the sweep-ings of racing stables, packaging the mixture in little bags and selling them to health food shops. I cannot be *sure* that this is what happened, of course. It is merely a hypothesis based on what the stuff looks like.

My wife actually likes it. But so do the cats and every breakfast sees a running battle between my wife and the beasts as to who gets most of her bowl of carthorses' delight. A week ago I had to put my foot down. I got used to the noise of the battle but the cats kept crashing through my newspaper from the other side, an unnerving surprise which had me soaring a foot in the air from a sitting position.

This morning my wife produced a huge carton of some new stuff for us to try as a substitute. It is called 'Huskies'. It looks, and I must say tastes, like roughly chopped-up corrugated cardboard, but the blurb on the packet says that it is made from cereal husks, which the company scientists have discovered contain everything the body needs.

I was crunching away at my first spoonful this morning when something horrible lodged itself in my throat. Something small, thick and hairy, like a dead bee. I did not panic. I took a deep breath through my nose and tried to dislodge it by screaming. My wife thought she might be able to hook it out with a wire coathanger and ran to find one. I had a more scientific thought which I put into practice. We have a roller towel on the back of the kitchen door. I draped myself through the roller towel and balanced myself in it with my legs dangling out one side and my head and shoulders out the other. I then knocked the top of my head rhythmically on the floor.

Out of my throat dropped a tiny plastic caveman. He was short and fat and was clad in a skin of plastic imitation fur.

As I climbed out of the towel my eye caught the back of the carton. In large letters it proclaimed 'See Inside – Free Cavemen! Collect the Set! Found Your Own Fine Family of Furries!'

Do join us at breakfast one morning down here in Thorpe, Surrey. Help yourself to a brimming bowl of cereal.

But be warned. Progress has been made in breakfast foods:

There are Furries at the bottom of our carton.

One man's meat is another man's poison

Proverb

THERE was only one occasion in my life when I put myself on a strict diet and I can tell you, hand on heart, it was the most miserable afternoon I've ever spent. A Sunday it was, and I didn't even get up till going on quarter-to-two. This was because I'd been sleeping with Lady Pamela that Saturday night and when you're in bed with her you don't get much chance for any shut-eye.

Lady Pamela, I should explain, was a bitch. A Doberman Pinscher bitch, to be precise, belonging to the couple at Number 64 who'd asked us to look after her while they made one of their weekend visits to Scotland. (They always go up there once a year; nobody knows why, but the neighbourhood rumour, judging from the contents of their dustbin, is that it's to lay a wreath on the grave of Johnny Walker.) Well, I don't know how much you've had to do with Doberman Pinschers – it can't be less than I have – but this one, for all her enormous size, was of such surpassing cowardliness that she wouldn't sleep by herself. We had a try at leaving her down in the kitchen, but every time the fridge motor switched on, she went into moans of hysteria so wracking we had to feed her Good Boys dipped in brandy. So she wound up on our bed; though even there she had an attack of the quivering yelps when the Teasmaid went off.

So when I got up at midday, I was already suffering from the Redeye Headthuds and what made me feel even more irritable was that when Lady Pamela followed me into the bathroom I discovered in myself an uncharacteristic modesty about undressing in front of a strange dog. However, I couldn't very well shove her out because someone three doors away had just started up a vacuum-cleaner and she was already carrying on as though it was *The Invasion of the Body Snatchers*.

So I let her hang around, had my bath, dried myself on the non-guest towel then, as is my weekend wont, stood on the bathroom-scales. And that's where I received this well-nigh heart-stopping shock ... Since the previous Sunday I'd put on sixteen pounds!

Now I must explain I'd been very fortunate in that never in my life had I ever needed to worry about any kind of weight problem. While most of my contemporaries were now lunching on those diet biscuits that taste like tongue-depressors, then spending the rest of the hour wandering from shop to shop in search of shirts that taper outwards, I was still able to eat whatever I fancied and still get into a stock-size slim-fitting. Nevertheless I'd always nursed a secret fear that one day this happy state of metabolism would leave me; that, overnight, my body would suddenly develop some kind of immunity to being thin. So the moment I saw that dial-reading my immediate thought was 'It's happened!' Grabbing a bathrobe, I hurried down the stairs, shouting 'Here it *is*! The spread has come upon me! Overweight has arrived! Action stations!'

The announcement aroused a certain mild interest among the loved ones seating themselves for Sunday lunch, but nothing like the wild consternation I had anticipated. 'Don't you understand?' I screamed. 'This is the onset! My metabolic rate has upped itself to sixteen pounds in one week! By Christmas I'll be getting approaches from fairgrounds.'

'Do close that bathrobe,' my wife said, with a motion of her head indicating her mother's presence.

Was this to be their only reaction to the thunderbolt I had unleashed? 'If you think,' I said deliberately, 'that I'm just tamely going to allow it to happen, I must inform you that is not my way. From now on, gang – it's Diet Time!' With which, I grasped the trolley that held the Sunday lunch, ran it through to the kitchen, out the back-door and tipped the whole lot neatly into a dustbin.

That succeeded in focusing their attention on the problem. 'What the flaming hell are you playing at?' said my daughter. She was, if I remember correctly, three at the time.

So I sat down and told them about the one firm conclusion I have come to with regard to dieting. Contrary to popular opinion, the most uncomfortable aspect of it is not the continual need to watch what you eat. To my mind, the really difficult part is having to watch what other people are eating. 'Therefore,' I explained, 'if I'm to be obliged to cut out meals, so must everyone else. That way you will subject me neither to envy nor temptation. In other words, what I'm now calling upon you to display is that precious quality of family life called supportiveness.'

You know all that stuff you keep hearing on *Woman's Hour* about the British still deriving their strength from the intangible bonds which unite individual families? That Sunday I learned it's a theory to be taken with more salt than you'll find in a Cerebos warehouse. By four o'clock, my daughter had already been in touch with three different adoption societies. As for my son, my only male progeny, my posterity . . . frankly, it's something I still don't like talking about. You work your fingers to send them to a good school, give them all the advantages – and where do they end up? Out at the dustbin, using their bare hands . . .!

I'm still not sure whether I'd ever have regained my faith in the family as a viable unit, had it not been for my mother-in-law. Somewhere round half-past five, just after the couple from Number 64 had arrived, beaming and swaying, to collect Lady Pamela, she came over to me and whispered, 'I've been thinking.'

'Not as bitterly as I have,' I said.

'Please do something for me. Go upstairs and see what you weigh now.'

'Going without my lunch can't have made much difference.'

'You can never tell,' she insisted. Unwillingly, muttering savagely, I climbed the stairs again, threw off the robe and sceptically placed myself back on the fateful machine.

How many calories are there in humble pie? What I read on the dial sent me hurtling downstairs in elation. Throwing my arms round my mother-in-law, I cried, 'How did you *know*? It's gone! The whole sixteen pounds! What did it? What got rid of it? Was it merely doing without one load of roast potatoes and treacle tart? Or was it–' I swallowed hard – 'was it the energy-force that's only generated by the love of a close-knit family?'

'Neither,' she said. 'This time that animal didn't have its foot on the scales.'

I still say the manufacturers of those bathroom scales were the ones to blame. What kind of technology is it which allows its evaluation of human body-weight to be influenced by the intrusion of a great stupid dog? There is something very much to be deplored in a household machine where, as the old proverb hinted:

One man's meat is a Doberman's paws on.

'Tess of the D'Urbervilles'

Thomas Hardy
Title of novel

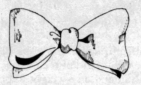

I'M worried about Fred.

You know. *Fred.* Of course you do. Fred Selmes? Comes and rearranges nature in our garden a couple of afternoons a week? Shortish? Widish? Can work for hours planting things with his legs straight and his forehead brushing the ground?

When I say I'm worried – I'm not really all *that* worried. I mean, nobody sleeps all that well at this time of the year and I don't really need much sleep. It's really a matter of face. Or rather, face: potential loss of.

He hasn't said anything, of course. But then he doesn't need to. The other morning, for instance, he asked me to give him a hand by brushing the leaves off the lawn preparatory to mowing. I immediately sprang into action with a brisk 'Can do, Skipper', nipped into the house, located the dustpan and brush in the cupboard-under-the-stairs and in a trice was down on my hands and knees on the lawn flicking the leaves into the pan like billy-ho. I looked up and there was Fred. Not saying anything. Just sort of staring at me. He was breathing a little strangely, I thought, and shaking his head slightly from side to side. I found it most unnerving.

When things are going well, i.e. when Fred has the garden to himself and I am not helping, he is the soul of fun, regaling us with stories of old village characters, chuckling away to himself. But when I take it upon myself to do a bit of gardening a change seems to come over him. He becomes markedly terse.

Like the *affaire* of the potatoes. I think that was the beginning of my loss of face with Fred. My wife needed some potatoes dug up. Fred was busy planting out (whatever that means). 'Taters,' he said to me. 'Would you mind?'

I selected a fork with which to dig and strolled through the kitchen garden, determined to locate the ripest bunch of potatoes available, two or three pounds of the little darlings at point of lay, each in its prime. I couldn't find any at all. I searched the ground, peered in the fruit-cage, inspected the trees. Not a spud to be seen. The kitchen garden was to all intents and purposes murphyless.

I was about to report the state of affairs to Fred when some sixth sense held me back. Instead, I slipped upstairs to consult my daughter, who was in bed with 'flu. With a few graphic phrases I sketched in my predicament.

'They grow underground,' said my daughter.

'Ah,' I said. 'That explains much.'

Back I went and peered round the kitchen garden. There was a bewildering choice of green vegetation to choose from. I experimented by digging up a random selection and harvested some onions, a carrot, an albino carrot which, with hindsight, I think must have been a parsnip, and a croquet hoop.

I returned to the bedroom and persuaded my daughter to wrap herself in the eiderdown and totter outside to point out to me exactly where the potatoes were. They lay below such nondescript foliage that I was not at all surprised that I had overlooked them. I plunged the fork downwards, heaved upwards and found the spikes covered with impaled potatoes. The fork looked like a weird four-decker vegetarian kebab. I removed the pierced potatoes with the edge of my boot and had another go. Same thing happened.

I sat down and had a big think. Clearly the potatoes had to be approached differently. By the side of the row of potatoes was some disused earth with bits of fern straggling over it. I took a spade and dug a long trench in it, about two feet wide and three feet deep. I then crouched down inside the trench and tunnelled sideways in the direction of the potato plants. I used a trowel for this so as not to pierce any more of the precious fruit. Sure enough, after a fair bit of tunnelling and scraping, I exposed a number of potatoes, hanging downwards from the roots. These I carefully pulled up – as it were, downwards. When I had finished, Fred appeared. He just stood there, looking at my trench, silent; but his Adam's apple was going up and down like a yoyo.

'New way of gathering spuds,' I said, breaking the silence after what seemed about an hour. 'Dug up this bit of waste here – nothing on it but fern . . .'

Fred spoke. With some difficulty. And quite quietly.

'That . . . was the asparagus bed,' he said.

After that he went terse for a month and life became unbearable.

It was the same after the *affaire* of the hose. Which, I still maintain, was not my fault. Fred wanted to do a bit of watering amongst the shrubs. This needed a fine spray which he first had to clip on to a gadget which then clipped on to the end of the hose. The hose was at its fullest stretch and the tap was round the corner of the house, out of sight of the shrubbery. Naturally I offered to switch the water on for Fred to save him marching back and forth. I asked him to call out when he was ready. The rose with the fine spray does not clip easily on to the gadget so Fred parked the end of the hose inside the waistband of his trousers while he struggled with it. He eventually got it on and let out a shout of triumph.

Put yourself in my position. I was out of sight, standing by the water-tap, and I suddenly heard Fred shout 'YES!' I turned the tap on.

No permanent damage was done, of course. All that really happened was that, as Fred's trouser bottoms were tucked into his wellies, his trousers filled with water and bulged out until he looked like a Dutchman. In a flash I plunged a pruning knife into the seat and he quickly deflated. And that was that.

Another month of terseness before he returned to normal.

Now perhaps you can understand why, after nearly three months of the happy, chatty side of Fred I am desperately anxious not to slip up on a little commission which he has asked me to undertake.

It was yesterday. He was sorting out plants and suddenly said to me, 'Dibber.'

Thinking he was giving me the old Boy Scout greeting, I replied suitably, 'And dib, dib, dib to you!'

He closed his eyes for a moment and then went on, 'I need a dibber. By Friday if possible.'

I said, 'I know what a dibber is, of course. Who doesn't, ho-ho! But – what precisely do you want it for? If you know what I mean . . .'

'To put seeds in, of course. And bulbs.'

'Righty-ho!' I said. 'You shall have your dibber. By Friday.'

I rushed to the dictionary. Do you know what a dibber is? According to my dictionary a 'dibber' is a kind of fishing-rod used when you fish by trailing the bait across the surface of the water. Well, if that's what he wants. I rushed into Egham and bought a long, whippy bamboo pole, about eight feet long.

If he was going to use it, as he said he was, to put seeds in, then presumably he would stick it in the earth so as to have his seeds near at hand. And he would need containers for the seeds. I rushed back to Egham and bought a dozen little plastic bags. These I nailed to the pole at intervals, labelling them, for his convenience, Potato Seeds, Mushroom Seeds, Daffodil Seeds, etc.

What was the other thing he needed the dibber for? Ah yes – bulbs. Presumably so that he could garden by night. I rushed back to Egham, bought half a dozen hundred-watt bulbs, half a dozen sockets and fifty yards of flex. I screwed a cross-bar to the pole and wired up the bulbs along it. To finish the whole thing off I painted it red and tied a pink bow to the tip.

It is undeniably a fine dibber. I would go further and say it is a beautiful dibber. But the point is, will it at last convince Fred that I know quite a bit about gardening and am not just a poop with a nincom? All will be revealed tomorrow when I give it to him. Which is why I am so worried.

He will be his old, happy self for the next three months if the dibber succeeds. But . . .

Terse if the dibber fails.

He who hesitates is lost

Proverb

WHEN I was sixteen, going on seventeen, if you'd have asked me what my greatest immediate ambition was, I'd have said, 'To write a large exclamation-mark in my diary.' What made such an objective even more remarkable was that, for a large part of that period, I had no idea what the exclamation-mark was supposed to signify.

All I knew was, one Monday morning soon after that school term began, a friend of mine called Snitch Herman entered the classroom, beckoned some of us to him and, looking around to make sure we were unobserved, exhibited his diary. There, on the page for the Saturday just past, he'd written a large red exclamation-mark. It was followed by the words, 'Approx 10.45 p.m. In shed on her father's allotment.'

'Cor!' Weedy Forbes said, in a hushed voice. (We called him Weedy because he was so painfully skinny it was claimed he could climb into a polo-neck sweater from either end.) 'Cor!' said Weedy, 'that makes you the first one in the class!' Snitch's only response to that was a smirk, but I noticed that as he went to his desk, his walk had acquired a definite swagger.

By that dinner-hour the news was buzzing round the whole school. 'Did you hear about Snitch on Saturday night? Cor!' Caught up in the general excitement, I even began retailing it myself. 'Did you hear about Snitch?' I said, grabbing another friend of mine called Wally Beckman. 'Last Saturday night at 10.45. Cor!'

'Not an exclamation-mark?' said Wally hoarsely. I

nodded. 'Cor!' he said, and it was clear from the admiration in his eyes that I had acquired kudos by merely conveying the information. This even though I still had not the faintest idea what I was talking about.

The following Monday it was Puffy Layton's turn. 'I'm the second in the class!' he shouted as he entered. And, sure enough, there in his Hobbies diary, flanked by the words, '9.17 p.m. – inside Out Of Order telephone box' was another large, triumphant exclamation-mark. Over the next few weeks one after another of my fellow students came into school brandishing their various diaries. By half-term no less than fifteen out of my class of thirty had uttered their cries of 'I'm twelfth!', 'I'm fourteenth!' then flushed and grinned at the congratulatory whoops it evoked.

It was obvious that some kind of race was in progress.

Equally obvious was the status one attained by reaching its mysterious finishing-line. So if I was ever to share that status, it looked like I'd have to file my own qualifying round pretty soon. But what sort of race was it? And what did you have to *do* to qualify?

My ignorance was only dispelled when I was allowed to read the considerably more specific details added in tiny writing beside the exclamation-mark which Wally Beckman ('I'm seventeenth!') had awarded himself. It was all to do with – oh, no! – persuading *girls*! In effect our diaries needed to become what would nowadays be known as score-boards. What's more, at the rate at which the ones belonging to my peer-group were achieving that conversion, unless I started exercising persuasion on someone within the next two weeks, end-of-term would see Weedy Forbes and me dead-heating for last place.

My heart sank. When it came to exerting power over the opposite sex, I'd already discovered that I had neither the silver-tongued quick-wittedness of a Snitch Herman – his exclamation-mark had been achieved by convincing a girl in Form V that the captain of a cricket-team could perform marriages – nor the uncaring brutality of a Puffy Layton. ('You might as well. I'll tell everyone you did anyway.') In fact, I had long ago resigned myself to the probability that in the same way that a hero of those days had become known as The Man Who Never Was, I would probably end my life as The Man Who Never Did.

My one source of hope looked to be Bessie Arkwright. She was the only girl I'd ever met who seemed to prefer being in my company to going home and helping her mother unblock the sink. The reason I hadn't yet responded to the unspoken invitation in her eyes was because – how can I put this kindly? – she had the configuration of a born ice-hockey goalkeeper. To phrase it more bluntly, she was built in the way they used to build cars at that time – all the weight at the back. Nevertheless, I had taken her out a few times, mainly because she was the only girl I could get with the kind of suits my parents had bought me that summer. Besides that, though, not only was she enthusiastically disposed towards me, but her father owned the local cinema, so she was cheap to run.

One could therefore sum up our relationship so far by saying that although it had the right chemistry, up to this time there has been no signs of biology. Now, however, with no more than a fortnight to go before the end of term, Bessie suddenly became my only exclamation-mark hope.

That's why the very next Saturday night found us in the back row of her father's cinema, with me making ardently unsuccessful attempts to practise what might be called 'slide of hand'. Immediately after the big film, which she hadn't actually seen that much of, owing to some trouble getting her glasses on over newly-acquired false eyelashes, I set in motion the next step of my carefully prepared plan. Hurrying her to the milk bar, I plied her with double-strength strawberry shakes. The moment she began gazing at me with that familiar misty look, I called for the bill and rushed her back to her house before my scented cachous lost their potency.

Once installed on her couch, I went to action-stations, 'Bessie,' I said, 'come and sit on my lap.'

'Why?' she said, lost in some romantic dream.

Drawing a deep breath, I gave it to her straight across the bows. 'Because,' I murmured with painstakingly rehearsed fervour, 'you and I could make beautiful exclamation-marks together.'

She rose from her chair. 'All right then,' she said – and dropped into my lap.

Now, one belief that was unquestioningly accepted by all pubescent youths of those days was that girls judged your charisma by the number of keys you had on your key-ring. So bearing in mind what I've already told you about the way Bessie's body-weight was distributed, do you really need a detailed description of what happens when a girl of that build drops into the lap of a lad carrying a bunch of twenty-two keys in his trouser-pocket?

I'll content myself with saying that as far as the Exclamation-Mark Stakes were concerned, I was forced to retire hurt. To such an extent, in fact, that two kids from the Lower Third got their diaries marked before I did.

But even more humiliating, perhaps, was the jeering message I received from Weedy ('I'm twenty-ninth!') Forbes. Scrawled across the front of his get-well card were the words:

'He who Bessie dates is last.'

One good turn deserves another

English proverb

H ELLO, children!
Are you all sitting comfortably? If you are, shuffle about
a bit otherwise you might go to sleep. That's better. If you
are all sitting reasonably uncomfortably, but alert, I will
begin.

It is a story of unrequited love in the depths of a fairy
wood. A nature story of the Great Outdoors. It has to be an
outdoor story because that is where nature is, on the
whole. In fact, apart from a few Chicago Ivy plants and an
onion-like hyacinth bulb dying in a jam-jar on the kitchen
windowsill, I cannot think of much nature going on
indoors.

The scene of our story is a forest clearing by the banks of
a river; an enchanted spot which the animals called 'Never-
Never Land'. Nobody knew why it was called Never-Never
Land but the wise old owl thought it was because the little
ducklings in the water kept warm by a little down every
week. And the parrots lived on higher perches.

Some of the birds and the beasts and the fish and the
insects and the – whatever else hangs about forest glades –
were very happy living in their little homes by the river and
as the sun went down at twilight, the glade would ring with
merry laughter and the sharp cries of wild things greeting
each other.

Trout shouted 'Toodle-pip!'

The carp (which cheers but not inebriates) cried 'Chee-
rio!'

Molluscs murmured 'Morning!'

And salmon chanted 'Evening!'

But all was not peace and beauty in that lovely dell. Oh, my goodness, no. As the poet wrote (but forgot to rhyme) 'nature in the raw is seldom mild'. Several small, furry and finny things were not at all happy. For instance, Beatrice the Bunny was madly in love with Vincent the Vole. All day long they mooned about in the long grass holding paws and sighing and gazing into each other's eyes – a complicated business as their eyes were on either side of their heads rather than in front so they had to keep dashing round each other to gaze into the loved one's other eye, only to find that the loved one was on the way round to do the same.

But worse than that, they had to do their courting in full view of all the other animals. This was because the woods were full of evil hunters with guns who were on the lookout for game to make into potted meat to sell to West Germany. And Vincent and Beatrice were prime targets. In the words of the wise old owl, 'A vole and his bunny are soon pâtéd.'

And there was Terence the tadpole who was so looking forward to growing up and turning into a butterfly that nobody had the heart to tell him that he had got it wrong.

And there was the other little water creature who lost all his money playing poker with a group of leopards (one of them turned out to be a cheetah) and spent every evening singing to himself and falling into the river. He was Titus, a newt.

However, the saddest of all the animals in the clearing was Starkers the otter. He was not always called Starkers. His real name was Tarka, but he moulted. Now say what you will, I maintain that there is no more unhappy a sight in outdoors nature than a bald otter. Starkers looked dreadful without his sleek, mink-like coat. It just did not look right for him to go around clad only in his pink skin. It was a shock to the system, like suddenly coming face to face with a policeman in a ballet skirt, or Miss Barbara Cartland in jeans and a T-shirt.

All the other animals were kindness itself to Starkers, never mentioning his affliction in case it gave him pain, always the soul of tact, ever seeking to cheer him up. 'Hey,

Baldy!' one would shout. 'Coming to the pub tonight?' Or 'Care to come as my guest to the Fancy-Dress Dance? Don't bother to change – just come as a skinned rabbit.'

But for all their efforts, Starkers sank deeper and deeper into gloom. He began to avoid the company of the other animals, even refusing to go with them into the forest on the annual orang outing. He would spend all day up a lonely creek of the river blowing his cheeks out until his eyes popped, trying to force his hair to grow.

Now Starkers had a friend. It was his cousin Geezer, a water-otter. Geezer became so upset at his friend's un-happiness that he went to consult the wise old owl. This he did not decide to do lightly, as besides being wise, the old owl was a crashing bore, but something had to be done.

'Why, wise old owl, is Starkers starkers? There must be a reason his coat fell off. Did he grow too fast and burst through it? Could he have run under a lawn-mower with-out noticing? Has he contracted otter-rot?'

The wise old owl held up a wing for silence and nearly bored the tail off Geezer for an hour, chuntering on about the need to keep the forest tidy and not to drop toffee-papers on the grass and there's far too much larking about in the tree-tops after dark and always leave the waterhole as you would wish to find it. Then he went on, 'I'm surprised you haven't asked me about your friend Starkers. Haven't you ever wondered why he's bald?'

'Yes, you stupid fowl,' muttered Geezer under his breath, 'I've just asked you!'

'Interesting case,' went on the owl. 'Quite simple, really. He's lonely. Needs a mate. So all his hair has fallen out. There is just one thing he needs to do and his hair will grow in again.'

'Just one thing he needs to do?'

'Just one thing,' said the owl. 'To wit – to woo.'

He was right, too. And here our story takes a happy turn before its sad ending. A few days after Geezer had seen the wise, boring old owl, Starkers fell in love.

She was not only, to his eyes, an otter of beauty. She was also as bald as he was. Entranced by her quiet, nay silent, charms he spent all day, every day, alone with her up his remote little creek of the river. And the more he wooed her

44

the more his hair grew until – and this is the happy bit – his coat was once more as sleek and glossy as it ever was.

We now come to the sad bit. Misty-eyed with love, poor Starkers had not seen things too clearly. What he took to be a beautiful, bald lady otter drifting downstream into his arms was not an otter at all. It was not even a live animal.

A few days previously a band of hunters had made camp upstream, feasting and carousing as was their wont. At one point in their proceedings they found that the gourd in which they kept their wine had a tear in it and was leaking so they flung it into the river. Vaguely animal-shaped, and completely bald, it had drifted downstream . . .

The whole tragic occurrence was summed up in the following morning's newspaper headline:

Wine-Gourd, Torn, Deceives an Otter.

Here today, gone tomorrow

Proverb

MOST of the items in my collection of show-business memorabilia are of minor historical interest – a custard pie once worn by Buster Keaton; the black wig that Betty Hutton put on to make Sonny Tufts think she was Rosemary Lane in *Here Comes The Waves*; a flower from the bouquet Dana Andrews gave Anne Baxter in *Crash Dive* (little realizing she was already in love with Tyrone Power). But one item that does offer a modicum of sociological value is a collection of reports sent back to England by the ringmaster of a small travelling circus while it was touring Europe in the early fifties. They are all addressed to the circus's owner, who appears to have exercised his proprietorial role from a small suite of rooms at the surgical appliances end of Charing Cross Road. I append a selection herewith:

15 November, northern Spain. Another exhausting overnight journey, this time from Mannheim, West Germany, where I'm afraid business was not as brisk as expected. Our box-office takings, like the breezes that unexpectedly blew our Big Top down, were light and variable. As a consequence of the tent's collapse, we were obliged to give the rest of the week's performances in the open air, a circumstance which played havoc with several of our star acts, particularly Supremo, The Human Cannon Ball. Unaccustomed to adjusting his trajectory for wind-deflection, Supremo had the misfortune to crash into a low-flying aircraft.

We had to leave him in Mannheim General Hospital and although I am advertising in the Pamplona papers for a man to take over his act, I fear it will be difficult to find a performer of his calibre.

22 November, central Italy. I really must register my misgivings about the zig-zag manner in which you appear to have routed this year's venues. We had the utmost difficulty making the journey from Pamplona on Saturday night in time to open here in Assissi by five p.m. on Monday. For any circus which includes a travelling menagerie, such non-stop dashes through the night on minor European roads present a multitude of problems, particularly in the matter of low bridges. We arrived here minus yet another giraffe – a tragedy which, I can assure you, has not made for good relations with the Assissi Chamber of Commerce.

Takings at Pamplona were up somewhat on the preceding week, thanks mainly to the resourcefulness displayed by Ram Das Jamshid, Mystic Eastern Snake-charmer. In an endeavour to liven up business, he advertised that, Second House Saturday, he would perform his snake-charming routine with – for the first time in any ring – no less than three poisonous cobras, all of whom were absolutely stone-deaf. Such showmanship reflects nothing but credit on Mr Jamshid, who would have been thirty-eight next Tuesday.

29 November, southern Norway. If the journey from Assissi to Stavanger proved less hectic than had been anticipated, put that down to the unfortunate fact that we were unable to play out the full week there, being obliged to depart first thing Wednesday morning. This was because certain sharp-eyed members of Tuesday night's audience spotted that one of Madame Zorba's Team of Magnificent Arabian Liberty Horses was, in fact, stuffed.

You will recall that when I phoned you last September from Lisbon to convey the news of the animal's demise, you made the suggestion that rather than go to the expense of a replacement I should come to a discreet arrangement with a good local taxidermist. As I later reported, he turned out to be an expatriate Englishman called Nigel Deames who, apart from a tendency to make distasteful remarks about 'taking a dead Liberty', performed his duties so admirably that until last week no spectator had commented.

However, Tuesday First House, even though we maintained our usual precaution of bringing the inanimate animal into the ring while the tent was darkened, murmurs were heard when the spotlights came on again. When, a little later, Madame Z's splendid pretence of feeding it a lump of sugar after leaping off its back brought a group of Assissi priests surging over the barrier, I thought it best to de-rig and start north.

In this same connection, I have been asked to relay a request from another of our attractions, Buffalo Cyril Cody – the stellar half of Cody & Bessie, Western Knife Throwers Extraordinaire. Having had the misfortune to suffer a sudden power blackout right at the most dramatic moment of their act, Mr Cody would now like to know whether, instead of wasting time auditioning for a new Bessie, you would prefer him to get in touch with Mr Nigel Deames again?

6 December, Austria. May I once again touch on the matter of inconvenient routing? Our journey from Stavanger to our present location in Graz meant travelling, according to my pedometer, more than 800 miles. That really does seem an inordinate distance to come for a one-night stand, especially as we are booked to appear in the south of France tomorrow night.

If my reports seem to harp unduly on this point, it is because one effect of such arduous and prolonged journeys is that more and more pieces of equipment vital to artists' performances are getting either damaged or mislaid. It cannot but detract from the glamour of a circus when, as happened tonight, an audience sees a daredevil tight-rope walker walking a high wire which has had to be tied in the middle with an improvised granny knot.

There were equally disillusioning consequences when the special-sized swords used by Largo, our Midget Sword Swallower, were found to have disappeared somewhere in transit. As a result, the poor little fellow was obliged to give his performance tonight using hastily borrowed substitutes from the Stavanger Museum of Viking History. Although the very smallest of these was over four feet in length, not only did Largo succeed in getting it down as far as the embossed handle, he might have gone on to complete his act had not the applause induced him to try to take a bow.

However, trouper that he is, he insists on coming along with us to the south of France date tomorrow, claiming that we can still make use of him in some capacity, if only as a tent-peg.

13 December, the south of France. This really is the last straw! When we arrived at our site this morning, after a journey across the Alps of such nightmare dimensions that Elasta, the Amazing Lady Contortionist, still cannot be persuaded from the caravan where she lies sprawled across a bunk sobbing hysterically into the small of her back, what did I find? A letter from you, addressed Post Restante, Hyères, informing me that you have donated our services to a charity gala to be held tomorrow afternoon in central Belgium!

I regret having to tell you this, but when I conveyed that information to our artists and roustabouts, their unanimous reaction was 'We Shall Not Be Moved!' Pamplona to Assissi they could understand; Assissi to Stavanger they were ready to accept; Stavanger to Graz was complied with and they even agreed to the overnight safari from Graz to Hyères.

But if there is one journey which even the great warm heart of circus folk will balk at, it is the itinerary with which we are presently confronted:

Hyères today, Ghent tomorrow.

Dirty British Coaster with a salt-caked smoke stack

John Masefield
'Cargoes'

To my generation, that line of Masefield's must be the best-known line of poetry in the English language. In Broadstairs we grew up with it ringing in our ears. If we were nabbed by a constable riding away from school on a bicycle with a wobbly saddle we were required to recite 'Dirty British coaster with a salt-caked smoke stack' faultlessly or were booked for not only riding a bicycle with a wobbly saddle but also for being drunk in charge of a bicycle with a wobbly saddle.

In those careless, carefree years of the nineteen-twenties and thirties we flung ourselves recklessly into the business of living. Our life seemed to be one continuous round of beach parties, some of them going on far into the night until half-past ten or a quarter to eleven. And one of our favourite games was a kind of Russian Roulette. We all ate three Jacob's Cream Crackers and then tried to say 'Dirty British coaster with a salt-caked smoke stack'. The first one to spit crumbs was whacked with a rolled-up copy of *Razzle*.

By what strange metaphysical alchemy did Masefield conceive that one line, so powerful that it shaped a generation? So versatile that it was readily pressed into service as a breathalyser and as an activator of crumb-spitting?

These are not easy questions.

To find the answers we have to delve deep into Masefield's past and the psychological and physical background to the poem.

The first significant fact we find is that Masefield was

married when he wrote the poem. But far more interesting to us is the fact that, in spite of the social attitudes prevalent at the turn of the century, Masefield's was a mixed marriage. He was a man and his wife was a woman. As we follow the progress of the marriage it becomes clear that his wife was a great inspiration to him in his work.

One Tuesday morning we find him in the breakfast room contemplating his breakfast without much enthusiasm. He has a slight cold. This may not be of importance to us but it was to him because it meant he could not smell his porridge and he liked the smell of porridge better than its taste. Without the smell it always seemed to him to be like warm, sodden confetti. What does concern us is that he lacked one poem to finish a new book and was not getting far with it. Deep in unproductive thought, he filleted a kipper, ate the bones and piled the fish at the side of his plate.

In zoomed Mrs Masefield, bright as a button, carrying a pork pie and a flagon of rum for her friends Mr and Mrs C—, who were unwell (*Note:* Humbert Clitheroe and his wife Tetty. They lived at the foot of the hill and were old friends of the Masefields).

'Sorry to leave you alone, dear,' she said, 'But it can't be helped. I must go down to the C—s again.'

Masefield's eyes flickered. 'Make that "seas",' he thought to himself. 'I must go down to the seas again.' He pondered. 'Could be something there but not a winner, I fancy.' He looked up.

'You can't go,' he said. 'Car won't start.'

'It will for me!' she riposted, with a wave of her basket.

Sure enough, she had only to adjust the advance lever on the steering wheel, turn the petrol on and give the handle a quick upward pull and the Austin Seven twitched into life. Mrs Masefield went back to the house, put her head through the (open) window of the breakfast room and announced, 'Car goes!'

'*That's* the title I've been searching for!' he cried. 'Cargoes!'

Absently peeling a boiled egg, he ate the shell with a spoon and piled the egg neatly at the side of his plate, his fertile poet's imagination busy fertilizing. 'Cargoes. Three different sorts of boats and cargoes, I think.'

He began to make notes on a piece of toast.

'Piglead, ivory, peacocks – what else do ships carry? – apes, firewood . . .'

But somehow the poem would not come together. He made one false start after another.

'A dirty old ship with one funnel,
   Was laden with apes to the gunwale,
   Plus Palestine wine,
   Cheap coal from the Tyne . . . No, too ordinary a metre. I need something more tumty-tumty-tumty-tumty-tum-tum-tum-tum.'

All day he worked but the one magic line which would set the metre of the poem eluded him.

His wife did not return until the early evening. With a woman's intuition she sensed, from the fact that he was still in his pyjamas and the room was knee-deep in rolled up bits of paper, that he was working so she sat down quietly to read the evening paper. Not really aware that she was speaking aloud, she read out the headline.

'That's *it*!' shouted Masefield. 'That's the line I have been searching for all day! The key line of the poem! Read it again!'

Mrs Masefield looked at the headline. And the picture beneath it. Deeply interested by now, she read the whole story.

The year was 1930 and the British film industry had started to shoot the first British musical, to the excitement of the press and the British public.

The film was to be called *Mayfair Lady*. It told the story of a little flowergirl in Covent Garden who is taken up by an Italian Mafia boss. He teaches her to speak with an Italian accent with the intention of setting her up in Mayfair as a high-class foreign tart. But he falls in love with her instead. He takes her to Ascot races to test her accent but accidentally falls in front of the king's horse and the film ends with her marrying the young man who has been in love with her all along, George Bernard Shaw.

The star of the film was the great Italian tenor Beniamino Gigli. He had most of the big songs, like 'Why Can't a Woman Be More Like a Horse', 'I've Thrown a Custard in Her Face' and 'Get Me to the Judge on Time'.

His co-star was the vivacious British *ingénue*, Lottie Lucas, known to film fans as the Gin-and-It Girl. Lottie, if not actually certifiable as off her chump, was distinctly dotty. She had been divorced at the age of seventeen by her first husband, an earl, who had cited forty-two co-respondents, including five footballers (mostly Third Division), a gondolier and the front-of-house manager of the Electric Kinema, Dalston Junction. One of her little peccadilloes was, when bored, to break into an extremely rapid Charleston dance, wherever she happened to be, e.g. at her first husband's funeral.

It seems that the film company had been shooting a key scene that day on the jetty at Broadstairs. It was the scene where Eliza Dottle (Lottie Lucas), unable to master the Italian language and at her lowest ebb, had decided to run for it. She has disguised herself as a peasant by donning a heavy Breton smock and is just about to hitch a lift in a fishing-boat to France when after her, along the jetty, belts Gigli.

All had gone well with the shooting until after lunch when Lottie, stiff with Gin-and-Its, became bored with hanging around the jetty waiting for her next shot and broke into a fierce and swift Charleston. Her left foot caught in a coil of rope and the next moment she was wallowing in the water, yelling for help.

There was no real danger. There was a little donkey-engine near with a basket which was lowered into the fishing boats to land their catch. It was started up and Lottie managed to scramble into the basket. The donkey-engine chuffed away and Lottie rose slowly out of the sea. And then, eight feet up in the air, pouring out sea-water and swaying slightly, the basket – and Lottie – stuck.

The trouble was that it was only a very tiny donkey-engine, designed to lift fish. A heavy Breton smock full of sea-water and Lottie was another matter. The donkey-engine wheezed and died. And Lottie dangled.

And that was the scene which a photographer snapped and which the evening paper published.

Her husband's voice broke into Mrs Masefield's reveries. 'What was that headline, again?' His poetry-writing pencil hovered over paper.

Obediently she read it out:
'Dotty British Co-Star with a Salt-Caked Smock Stuck.'

'Luck, Be a Lady Tonight'

Frank Loesser
Popular song

'DOCTOR, you've got to find a way to help me.' The speaker was a shortish, middle-aged man with a look of uneasy jauntiness, like those minor relatives who swarm on at the end of *This Is Your Life*.

I surveyed him joylessly. Although this was only my second evening on Casualty Ward, I'd already made up my mind to jack in being a doctor. Whatever the practice of medicine may have done to provide Somerset Maugham with short-story material, it obviously wasn't going to be much help with my literary career. How can anyone jot down significant human insights when he's heaving and fainting all the time?

The little man broke into my reverie. 'Fact is, doctor . . .' His voice faltered, then dropped to a confidential whisper. 'It's my Prue.'

Automatically, my trained mind performed a rapid flip-through of *Gray's Anatomy*. Was that above or below the waist? Or was it – yet again – one of those parts of the body which, despite seven years of lectures, my brain still resolutely rejected the very idea of?

He solved the problem by going to the door and ushering someone in. 'My daughter,' he said.

Prue turned out to be the sort of docile heavily-built girl you could imagine being shared out among an undistinguished Hell's Angels chapter. She had a skin whose colours and texture resembled that of a baked rice pudding and everything below her neck was so unconfined that when her feet came to a halt, the rest of her took perceptibly longer to settle down.

Standing in front of me, she stared into my face. Not only was her gaze devoid of all expression but her lips were in continuous motion without any sound emerging. I took a step back, preferring to put a little more distance between us.

'Bloody Radio One,' her father said.

It took me some moments to establish the relevance of that comment to his daughter's condition. Then I noticed the thin white lead which was dangling from her right ear down to a bulky transistor set she was clutching to her stomach. 'She's listening to the radio?'

'Has been for three days and nights non-stop,' he replied gloomily. 'Earpiece won't come out. It's got stuck in.'

Moving to her side, I reached forward and gave the lead a tentative tug. Although nothing emerged from within the thicket of brandy-snap curls that insulated her ear, the movement turned her face back towards me. Again that empty stare.

Glancing at his watch, her father consulted a crumpled *Radio Times* he was carrying and shook his head despondently. 'It's *Your All-Time Top Forty*,' he said. He tossed the *Radio Times* on to my instrument trolley. 'Be no getting through to her now till News on the hour.'

He sighed. 'Point is, you see, she doesn't *mind* it being jammed in there. Doesn't want it out. She *likes* having continuous rock music, as it were, plumbed-in.'

Could that fact be a significant human insight? Just in case, I decided to essay the Maugham role of detached observer. 'I don't really think . . .' I began in as ironic a tone as I could manage.

Unfortunately he interrupted me. 'Say what you like, it's unnatural for a girl every time she undresses she's got to take her jumper off over her transistor. What I had in mind, you see, what I was hoping, was perhaps you could administer a swift anaesthetic, then prise it free while she's sparkers.'

My spirits fell again. Of all the parts of the human body a doctor is obliged to go grubbing around in, ears are among the least pleasant, especially after you've just washed your hands. Besides which, it would mean having to place that metal band with a light in it round my forehead, and I'd

56

not yet managed to do that without it falling over my eyes.

I decided to seek a second opinion. 'Would you excuse me a moment?'

Stethoscope swinging, I hastened over to the Ortho-paedic Ward, hoping to find the man who knew more about surgical procedures than anyone in the hospital. Luckily he was still in his Porter's cubicle. 'Tom,' I panted. 'Emergency. Narrow passage-way. Small object wedged in top of aperture. How to extract?'

He pondered. 'When we had it happen with the Nurses Home wastepipe, some bloke came and squirted water up from underneath.'

Good old Tom. But as I hurried back to Casualty I found myself assailed by doubts which, by the time I was facing Prue again, had hardened into certainty. Surely such a remedy was physiologically contraindicated?

So how to free this prisoner of pop? She was now swaying slightly, eyes closed, small moaning sounds audible. 'It's *The Clash In Concert*,' explained her father wearily, indicating the *Radio Times* he'd retrieved.

I ransacked my mind. Then, on a sudden impulse – or it could even have been a significant human insight – I took the magazine from him and flicked back a few pages. Luck was with me!

Uttering a few words of silent prayer, I picked up my No. 4 forceps and, grasping them firmly, reached forward to Prue. Seizing hold, I performed one deft, sideways movement.

Abruptly her swaying ceased. There was about ten seconds of silence. Then from her lips came the most anguished wail of desolation I have ever heard a human emit. Clapping a hand to the side of her head, she wrenched out the earpiece, flung it from her and collapsed into her father's arms. 'That was awful, Dad,' she sobbed. 'It was *agony*!'

Clasping her to him, her father looked at me accusingly. 'What did you do to my girl?'

Sometimes it is best to tell the patient the truth. I broke it to him as gently as I could. 'I switched her over to Radio Three.'

His jaw dropped. '*Classical* music?'

57

'A performance of *Iphigenia in Tauris*.'

There was a moment's pause, then he reached forward and wrung my hand. 'Thank you, doctor.'

'Don't thank me,' I said. 'Thank the composer of that opera for answering my silent prayer.'

For, indeed, it was he to whom I'd addressed my words when, noticing his work billed for that hour in the *Radio Times*, I had offered up that mute entreaty:

Gluck, free a lady tonight.

I am monarch of all I survey

William Cowper
Verses supposed to have been written by
Alexander Selkirk

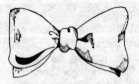

THE last three weeks have been a nightmare.
The house is awash with maps, dictionaries of quotations,
dictionaries of biography; vicars have been hurried in, consulted and hurried out again; telephone directories have
been studied; bibles have been sent for . . .

We are trying to find a name for our new kitten.

Constant readers of these reminiscences will know that this
household already supports an ageing Afghan hound named
Casanis (after a Corsican drink seemingly blended from
liquorice and torpedo fluid) and two Burmese cats, Mon-
ticello (after a small Corsican village) and Kettering (after
a large Northamptonshire town where a nice publisher
lives), and naming them took a month apiece.

Then my daughter acquired this new kitten.

Cuddles? Yuk. Fred? Nooooo. Bardolph? Gnaah. Milla-
mant? Urrrr. Spot? Bah. Gwen? Owwwww . . . far into the
night we argued and suggested and made noises of disgust
at each other's suggestions. Tempers frayed. A vase nar-
rowly missed my ear when I put up 'Tweedles'. Over
breakfast I came up with what I thought was a winner.

'Listen everybody!' I cried. 'It came to me in the night –
Wolverhampton!'

I am not sure quite why the name was unacceptable to my
family because I did not hear much of the subsequent discussion – I was at the sink washing home-made marmalade out of
my hair – but it was clear to me that I had soon to make a

59

political initiative if the family unit was to survive.

'The kitten will stay with me in my study for a week,' I said quietly but firmly. 'During which time I will observe it closely; its mannerisms, its personality, its physical appearance. From this data I will produce an apt and fitting name. This will be accepted by you all without demur, discussion or heaving jars of marmalade at me.'

All began to shout at once.

I held up my hand.

'I have spoken,' I said, with dignity. And ran for it.

It was a funny old week, looking back on it. The kitten and I got on well, on the whole, although I did not see much of her; she spent most of the working day up the back of my sweater. Not *all* day, of course, or she might have become bored. She usually spent the first half hour looking out of the window from her vantage point on top of my head. Quite why she took to sitting on top of my head escapes me. One would have thought that a shoulder would have been more comfortable but kittens – if I may be forgiven a generality – do not think logically. It was all right when I was typing because there was very little head movement and she could sit up there like a yellow sphinx, beadily eyeing the pigeons. It was more unsettling when the phone rang. To answer I had to swing my head round which meant that the kitten had to unsheath her scimitars and get a purchase on my skull. Most phone calls that week were answered by me with a brisk, 'Hello – six two seven five AAAAH!'

After half an hour the kitten would leap lightly down on to the keyboard of my typewriter – which meant that the beautiful prose which I was composing would then go $1\frac{3}{8}$ $2 = ns\frac{1}{24}\$ + \&b\%hr@$ – and make her way up the back of the inside of my sweater. There she would anchor herself firmly with four claws in my shirt and go to sleep indefinitely, leaving me with a profile like the late King Richard III or the French part-time bellringer, Quasimodo.

The kitten was clearly shy and hated to be moved from her nest and brought out to face the world, even for her lunch. It was all right when my wife was at home at midday, but on those days when she was away I had to trudge down to the gate and persuade a passing cat-lover to wrench the kitten out.

I had a girlfriend once who was as shy as the kitten. I was about fourteen at the time and a bit shy myself. Monica Willoughby, my lady love at that time, was of sturdy build. She too was fourteen and weighed in at twelve stone, including about a pound and a half of Everton toffee which she habitually carried on her person. Monica's shyness took the form of a change of colour in her face when addressed by somebody not of her immediate family. Her normally sallow, olive complexion would change to a shiny shade of beige with embarrassment, and then turn bright scarlet. It was like having a traffic-light for a girlfriend.

When the kitten was awake she talked all the time. 'Waaaah,' she went, 'Waaah, WAAAAAAAAAAH!' She reminded me irresistibly of another girl I knew in my youth, Val Valentine. Val chattered away happily every moment of her waking day. She never said anything; just talked. I took her to see Charles Laughton in *Mutiny on the Bounty* and she chuntered in a low voice throughout: '– I had a coloured shirt like Fletcher Christian's once – my aunty Bet gave it to me – I gave it away eventually – oh, look at that pretty beach! – ever been to Bognor? – I'd love to go to wassisname, the Barbados – I heard that Franchot Tone's mother was a French countess – would you like to finish my choc-ice? It's gone runny –' etc. We parted eventually. Not because of her chattering but because I felt she took too light a view of the charms of Clara Bow.

The kitten had a beautiful head of hair, a blonde mixture of apricots and cream. It reminded me irresistibly of the many happy hours I spent during the war cuddling Sergeant Baxter. Sergeant Lisa Baxter was a physiotherapist WAAF who gave me post-natal contraction exercises in the hospital where I had my appendix out. Lisa had striking blonde locks, much like the kitten's in hue, with a bit of black showing at the roots, which reminded me of the old French saying: 'At each parting we dye a little'. Our wartime romance was to be short-lived. I was posted away to convalesce at Blackpool and sent Lisa a sad little postcard, saying, 'Those blue lagoons, and tropic moons are nowhere near Blackpool, H. de Vere Stackpoole'. She did not reply. I heard later that she had been granted a compassionate posting to Iceland to await her hair returning to its natural colour.

Perhaps the most remarkable thing I observed about the kitten during that week was how clumsy she was. Most kittens race for an apple tree and run up it. My kitten ran at the apple tree but her head hit it with a sickening thud and she staggered away, semi-conscious. Again, ordinary kittens love leaping four feet into the air with *joie de vivre*. My kitten attempted this when under the kitchen table. She was only temporarily concussed but I can still hear that awful crunch of tiny skull on wood. The kitten's clumsiness brought to mind another girlfriend of my past, Fay Furness. Fay was not fat but she was, undeniably, a big girl. And beefy. She was hockey captain of her school when we met, but she was not allowed to bully-off because of the number of hockey sticks which she had snapped in two. When I went to Sunday tea at her home her mother would say 'Hand the cakes round, Fay. There's a good girl.' Fay would pick up the plate and swing it round. The plate would hit a small occasional table, demolishing it, and the cakes would fly across the room and thud into the wallpaper. Our romance came to an end when I went one day to Sunday lunch. I staggered away with crackling in my hair, an earful of apple sauce and a pint of gravy down my pullover.

Musing over the kitten's characteristics, it dawned on me that the problem of naming the kitten was solved. I would call it after the ex-girlfriend it most reminded me of. But which of the four was that? The shy one? The talkative one? The blonde-haired one? Or the clumsy one? Why not – I thought with a sudden flash of inspiration – all four?

I convened a family conference.

'I have a name,' I announced. 'A name which perfectly fits the kitten's general bearing and character. I will have a collar made for her, with a name tab. And, when she next runs up the drawing-room curtains and looks down on us with her usual expression of disdain, the name tab on her collar will proclaim:

'I am Monica Val Lisa Fay.'

N.B. The kitten turned out not to be a girl but a boy and my daughter has named him Lumio (after a Corsican village).

> Do not try to bite off more than you can chew

Proverb

THE whole rotten experience began when I received a notably terse letter from the manager of my bank, asking me to call in and see him with regard to my personal finances. I pitched up at his office sharp on the hour he'd designated and found him frowning over what I recognized as my bank pass-sheets.

After about four minutes of disapproving silence, he looked up from the documents. Narrowing his eyes, he said, 'Mr Norden, is this the very first time a bank-manager has called you in for an interview?'

'Yes,' I said. 'How did you know?'

He said, 'Because it's not necessary to undress.'

While I was buttoning-up again, he leaned back and put the tips of his fingers together. 'Well, now,' he said, 'your overdraft seems to have reached alarming proportions. Have you any explanation for that?'

I said, 'Well, not off-hand, no. It could have been this inflation all the chat-shows are on about. Or perhaps I diversified when I should have conglomerated. Who can say? You know how quickly money goes when you're enjoying yourself. No good worrying about it though, is it?'

His eyebrows shot up so fast I distinctly felt the air stir. He said, 'I'm afraid we are obliged to worry about it, Mr Norden. From the evidence of these accounts, what you seem to have been doing, if I may express it in a homely analogy, is earning money in Centigrade and spending it in Fahrenheit. Far from being able to afford your present life-style, you can't even run to the VAT on it.'

I must admit that up to that moment I hadn't even been aware that I had a life-style. I thought I'd just been living. But brushing aside my attempts to raise this interesting semantic point, he went on. 'There are some unpleasant consequences up to which we must now face.' Then he launched forth into a lengthy speech about 'credit-balance short-fall' and 'fixed term repayments' and 'secured interest arrangements'; a harangue of such earnest obscurity I felt the sides of my neck going stiff from attentive nodding. Only when he began using terms like 'eviction order' and 'bankruptcy proceedings' did I begin to realize what he was suggesting.

Aware that he'd attained the goal of alarm and despondency towards which he'd been striving, he leaned forward again with a little smile. 'In short,' he said, 'unless you effect sufficient domestic economies to write-off that overdraft within six months, you're down the tubes.'

To such an extent did that warning succeed in giving me the wind up, I couldn't wait to rush home and relay the news to my family. 'From now on,' I informed the dismayed faces gathered about me, 'your *vita* becomes a whole lot less *dolce*. Henceforth, it's goodbye the Nordens – hallo, the Waltons. This is Economies Time. As of today, the TV goes off sharp at ten, the car will only be used for going to places that are downhill, and for Sunday lunch the butcher will supply the cut of meat known as ankle of lamb.'

The next few months would have been grim indeed had it not been for the fact that, by one of those coincidences without which most of these stories would never even achieve lift-off, a leading women's magazine came out that week with a leading article called 'How We Can All Cut Down the Weekly Household Bills'. (You'll know the magazine I mean – it's the one that put its price up 10p the following issue.) And the main thrust of that important article was that in order to reduce household expenses, it is not necessary to deprive yourself of anything. 'Simply purchase *wisely*,' it said. 'Start going in for bulk-buying or mail order, or keep your eyes open for goods reduced in price because they're marked "Slightly Imperfect".'

Well, no one can say I didn't follow these three pieces of advice to the letter; but nor can it be said that any of them proved as cost-effective as was anticipated. There weren't many items being offered for bulk-buying round our way at that particular time and of those that were, I perhaps made the wrong choice. It could be that black pepper is not something the average family really needs to buy in bulk. Apart from the problem of where to store the sacks, my son has calculated it will take another four generations to work through the whole hundredweight. Neither have we yet found any really practical use for the twenty dozen used bicycle saddles and the four gross of condolence cards.

Something else I only learned by trial-and-error was that in the case of goods which are advertised at reduced prices because they are 'slightly flawed', it is advisable before purchasing to enquire as to the nature of the imperfection. Had I done that, it is unlikely that my wife would have had to find room in the attic for two dozen pillowcases with no openings in them, and six made-in-Paris bras, all of them cross-your-heart styling but each containing three cups. She also had stinging things to say about the twenty-five pairs of sheer stockings whose reason for being reduced to only 25p a pair was that they had the seams at the front. ('For that price,' I said when she pointed out the drawback, 'surely you can walk backwards.')

The matter of mail order purchasing led to another conflict of opinion. Although my family has still not allowed me to leave the house wearing the £18 suit I sent off for – made in Taiwan, and advertised as 'virtually indistinguishable from Savile Row tailoring' – I still believe that passers-by would have to be sharp-eyed indeed to notice that the fly is on the hip.

I don't want to give the impression that all our attempts at retrenchment were unsuccessful. I can wholly recommend using the mangle to squeeze the last drop of toothpaste out of the tube and, though it may appear to reach some new low in penny-pinching, affixing a rev-counter on the toilet-roll holder does achieve quantifiable results. (Strangely enough, cheese-paring didn't. Perhaps it just doesn't work on Camembert, but what we saved on cheese we had to spend on buying new razor-blades.)

So, you're probably now asking, what was the nett financial result of all this thrift? Well, I think it only goes to confirm what a car-dealer once told me – 'If you want economy, guv, you've got to pay for it.' When I went back to the bank manager after six months of the most determined and ingenious frugality, he had figures to prove that I was £600 deeper into the red than when I started.

The lesson, according to him, is that it's a waste of time trying to get your overdraft written off unless you are prepared to deprive yourself and family of such unnecessary luxuries as food, clothing and shelter.

Or, if I may express it in another of his homely analogies – Do not try to write-off more than you can eschew.

'The Miner's Dream of Home'

Music-hall song

> I saw the old homestead and faces I love,
> I saw England's valleys and dells.
> I listened with joy
> As I did when a boy
> To the sound of the old village bells.
> The fire was burning brightly . . .

It was when I set fire to our house that I realized how true the words of that beautiful old song were. And how inaccurate was the advice given in *The Householder's Vade-Mecum: A Thousand Hints, Tips and Wrinkles for the Home-Owner* (1928. 14th edn. Cover detached. Some spotting. Lacks Chap. 8. 1/9d.).

The older I grow – which I do annually, almost as a matter of routine – the more the scales drop from my eyes and I find that not only do the horses of instruction, which were the lodestones of my youth, turn out to be men of straw with feet of clay, but metaphors are not what they used to be either.

One after another of the old adages which I was brought up to believe have turned out to be false when put to the test. For example: 'Least said, soonest mended'. I took my car in for servicing recently. The clock needed mending. Nothing drastic, just an adjustment. On the way to the garage I remembered the old adage, which clearly indicated that the less I spoke, the quicker the clock would be mended, and resolved to be terse. I handed the keys to the service chap. '150,000-mile service, please,' I muttered briefly. 'And one other thing. Slow. Running too slow.

Adjust, please.' When I returned the following day I found the car in pieces. The engine had been dismantled and the entire garage staff was trying to find out why it was malfunctioning. Had I spoken in full and said that there was a small problem with the clock . . .

I grew up in the belief, handed on to me by the wise men of my tribe, that if you drop a slice of bread it always falls on to the carpet butter side down. A few years ago I tested the adage scientifically. I spread ten slices of bread thickly. I proceeded into the drawing room and balanced them on the up-turned palm of my right hand. With a powerful thrust of my right arm I hurled the slices into the air and observed the result. The real, true, figures were:

> 10 per cent hit me in the eye.
>
> 10 per cent hit the ceiling and stuck to it.
>
> 10 per cent hit the cat and stuck to it.
>
> 60 per cent dropped to the carpet butter side down.
>
> 10 per cent disappeared completely. Years later I found it in the springs underneath the sofa. How it got there is still a scientific enigma, as baffling in its way as the Bermuda Triangle.

Small wonder, then, that riffling through *The Householder's Vade-Mecum: A Thousand Hints, Tips and Wrinkles* a couple of years ago I noted, with some scepticism, advice therein that when you have a household fire, the greatest amount of damage is done not by the fire but by the major jet of water poured over your goods and chattels by the Fire Brigade. This hint, tip or wrinkle stuck in my mind because I was at the time experimenting with the truth of another adage remembered from my youth that there is no smoke without fire.

I had discovered that afternoon that there *is* smoke without fire. At least there is if you buy a small, conical, firework-like thing called a greenhouse fumigator and light the blue touchpaper. A few sparks appear, true, and creep down the blue touchpaper but they soon disappear and the thing begins to belch smoke. Acrid, nasty smoke which stings your eyes and makes you cough and drop it and have difficulty finding it again and then you cannot think where to put it.

At two o'clock the following morning I suddenly found myself wide awake. There was a smell in the house. I woke my wife and said, 'Can you smell something peculiar or is it just me?' She sniffed. 'Smoke! I can smell smoke!'

I rushed along the corridor and woke the children. 'Sorry to disturb you,' I said, 'but the house is on fire. Proceed in an orderly manner to a place of safety,' and rushed back.

'Don't keep rushing backwards and forwards,' said my wife. 'Ring for the Fire Brigade.'

'Never!' I shouted back. 'Did you not know that according to *The Householder's Vade-Mecum: A Thousand Hints, Tips and Wrinkles* the worst damage is not done by the fire itself but by the mighty jets of water poured over belongings by the Fire Brigade's hoses? The book says that the best treatment for household blazes is to stifle the heart of the fire with foam.'

'But we haven't got any foam,' said my wife, climbing wearily into dressing-gown and gumboots.

This was true and a bit of a poser.

I climbed reflectively into my own gumboots, brain ice-cold and racing.

'We'll make some!' I cried, in a flash of inspiration.

It is surprising how long it takes to find and gather together a few simple household requisites when your family is not in the mood to co-operate fully and cheerfully.

I found my daughter leaning up against the front door, fast asleep. I shook her awake and set her to work.

I found my son in the kitchen, eating cold roast potatoes from the refrigerator. I spoke to him warmly about rallying in a family emergency and sent him to find a bucket.

The smoke was getting very thick, and thickening, but we all assembled outside while I mixed my foam.

For what it is worth here is the recipe:

> Three partly used tins of bubble fluid, without bubble-blowing wire rings.
>
> A plastic bottle of dish-washing fluid.
>
> Half a cake of toilet soap.
>
> A sachet of something labelled 'Hollywood Stars Bubble-Bath – Free with *Over 21* Magazine'. We could not open the sachet so bunged it in whole.
>
> A packet of washing-machine powder.
>
> Half a bucket of water from the greenhouse water-butt.

I swirled the whole lot round in the bucket and it foamed happily, if a bit glutinously, and sought the heart of the fire. I could not find this so decided to hurl the foam through the back door. I had just done this when my wife suddenly said, 'The house isn't on fire.'

I said, 'What? *What?*'

She said, 'There is no flame. And the smoke is smelly. What did you do with that greenhouse fumigator you were mucking about with this afternoon?'

'*Experimenting* with,' I corrected, with dignity. 'It went out so I put it in the larder. At least, I *think* it went out. Come to think of it, there might have been just a *wisp* of smoke still curling from it . . .'

I left her thumbing through *The Householder's Vade-Mecum* under D for Divorce and stepped forward resolutely to retrieve the fumigator and hurl it somewhere out of harm's way.

I do not know whether you have ever stepped, in gumboots, on to a sea of foam over plastic tiles but I can assure you that the effect is instantaneous.

My gumboots seemed to shoot up so that for a split second I was horizontal, like an illusionist's assistant being levitated, then my head went down. There was a sharp 'crack' as my skull hit the floor, a blinding flash in my head, and I saw the old homestead and faces I love, and I saw England's valleys and dells, and I listened with joy, as I did when a boy, to the sound of the old village bells.

Which is why I maintain that the advice given for dealing with a fire in *The Householder's Vade-Mecum* is hopelessly wrong and that the old song is dead right.

It is not the great jet of water from the firemen's hoses which does the damage. It is something quite different:

The minor stream of foam.

'See What the Boys in the Back Room Will Have'

F. Hollander/Frank Loesser
Popular song

MOST people are aware that Johann
Sebastian Bach wrote more than a thousand musical com-
positions, but something I only found out recently was that
he also produced no less than twenty children.

I must say, it increased my respect for him no end.
Speaking as someone who also dabbles in writing stuff for
Radio Four's off-peak hours, I have some experience of
how difficult it is to create work of an enduring nature
when you've got progeny exchanging hammer-blows in an
adjoining room, even though there's only two of them in
my case. How Bach managed to turn out all those immortal
toccatas and capriccios with twenty of them belting each
other about I can't begin to imagine.

What's more, as all of us striving to produce art of lasting
importance are only too aware, nothing impinges on your
working hours like the minor distractions of parenthood.
Contrary to what sociologists would have us believe, the
most time-consuming interruptions are not provoked by
such issues as 'sibling-rivalry' or 'viable social interreact-
ing'. No, what parts you from your desk for really pro-
tracted periods are questions like 'Who had the scissors
last?' Just imagine how long it must have taken to sort that
one out when there were twenty-two denials to be cross-
examined.

As to that other daily problem, the regular morning
set-to regarding who should have the bathroom next, think
of how complex that becomes when you're twenty-two

in family. One musicologist I consulted maintains that the only way Johann Sebastian was able to solve it was by adopting the system that some launderettes use now – the issue of numbered tokens. He lent weight to the theory by pointing out that it would also explain why there's been so much argument regarding the sequential cataloguing of Bach's works. At some point the opus numbers obviously got mixed up with the bathroom rota.

What's more, that was by no means the only creative drain which Bach's fertility imposed on his genius. Has anyone ever considered the precious mental resources he must have expended simply in finding names for all those children? Although I've only had to do it for a mere two, I can vouch for the number of wasted working hours that are spent crouching over a dictionary of Christian names, muttering things like 'Well, Edwin means "Happy Conqueror".' 'Yes, but Robert means "Famous In Counsel".' So what must it have been like for someone who not only had twenty of them to label, but also a Mass in B Flat Minor to knock into shape before Christmas? In response to that question, my friendly musicologist could only offer me some inconclusive evidence that after the eleventh one Bach resorted to picking names out of the Yellow Pages.

But the major question I found myself asking was the financial one. How could this unique man, a father who probably had the bite put on him for more Smarties each Saturday than you and I shell out for over the course of a whole summer term, how could he afford to have no regular job and simply remain at home thinking up fugues and motets and the occasional Magnificat? Admittedly, he must have done very well from the Social Services – with that amount of progeny, they probably delivered the Family Allowance by Securicor – but just the same, there must have been quite a strain on the Bach finances. So how did he manage?

Well, that's where my musicologist directed me to the history books. According to most of the official biographies, the way in which this one-man population explosion assured himself of a steady growth in his current account was by hiring each of his children out to a member of the local aristocracy as either personal organist, Kappelmeister or Concert Master in Ordinary. (I didn't have time to look up exactly what that last post means, but I presume the holder of it must differ in some way from a Concert Master in Extraordinary, if only in certain personal habits.) What Johann Sebastian had been shrewd enough to realize was that the moment he had one solid chart-topper behind him – in the event, the Brandenburg Concerto – then for one of the local dukes or princelings to boast of having his own personal Bach in the drawing-room would be, in status symbol terms, the eighteenth-century equivalent of possessing an eight-track stereo.

That the results must have exceeded even his own expectations can be seen by what happened when Prince Leopold of Anhalt summoned him with the news that he was about to move into a new schloss. When he asked whether there was any chance of hiring a spare young Bach as family music tutor, Johann could afford to be quite cavalier. 'Sorry,' he said. 'They're all spoken for now. I've just promised the last one to the Duke of Weiner.'

Prince Leopold's face fell. 'I see . . . Any possibility you might have another one on the way?'

Johann shrugged. 'I really can't say. I haven't been home since this morning.'

There was no disguising the Prince's disappointment but your Hun does not give up that easily. 'Tell you what I'm prepared to do,' he said. 'Whatever the Duke has offered you for a lad, I'll not only match it pfennig for pfennig, I'll also commission two partitas and a suite.'

Bach reflected. Besides his having trouble with the Goldberg Variations, contrapuntal forms were passing out of style, Telemann's star was in the ascendant and that tailor was pushing for payment on the baroque overcoat. Prince Leopold, noting this indecision, was quick to press home his advantage. 'Why don't we talk further about it?' he said. 'How about lunch next Thursday? Tell you what – why not bring the family?'

And it was at this lunch that the Prince produced the remark which finally assured Bach's immortality. They all met at one of Saxony's most exclusive restaurants, where the head waiter conducted them to a table for twenty-three. 'Right then,' said the Prince as they sat down. 'What would everyone like to drink? . . . Frau Bach?'

'Nothing for me, thanks,' Bach's wife said. 'Not in my condition.'

Johann Sebastian's knuckles whitened. 'That being the case,' he said, 'make mine a double scotch.'

'How about the children?' asked the Prince. 'Herr Oberst, please go round and see what each of them would like.' Obediently the head waiter circled the table, taking orders for nine lemonades, seven fizzy oranges, two black-currant juices and one apfel-strudel. (That was Wilhelm Friedeman, the oldest but by no means the brightest; later died in poverty.)

Totalling up the children's requests, the head waiter said, 'That only comes to nineteen. Is one child missing?'

Johann Sebastian sighed. 'It always happens,' he said to the Prince apologetically. 'I *told* them to go before we left.'

'No matter,' said the Prince expansively. 'I'll have the waiter go in there and ask him.'

And, pointing an imperious finger at the door marked *Herren*, he gave the waiter the order which has resounded in musical history ever since:

'See What the Bach in the Boy's Room will have.'

> Too many cooks spoil the broth
>
> *Proverb*

HEREWITH absolutely everything there is to know about Scotland, its rainfall, exports, geographical features and history.

If you look at a map of Great Britain and take Britain as a chap in a very large hat riding a pig westward, then Scotland is his head down to his Adam's apple. Then you get Cumbria.

Rain certainly falls in Scotland (there are no recorded instances of it rising) but it also has a trick of hanging about in the air at about ear level. This phenomenon of white-coloured water suspended in the air around your face is known on the east coast as a 'haar'. This can be a trap to foreigners, e.g. the English, as it closely resembles the word 'ha' which is a 'hall'. Or it might be mistaken as part of the English word 'ha-ha' and taken to refer to half a sunken fence. In the Highlands it is referred to as a 'Scotch mist' but they usually try to pretend that it never happens so the word 'Scotch mist' is now applied to something which does not exist.

The traditional exports of Scotland are, in order of importance, whisky, whisky and whisky. Traditional minor exports have included such useful everyday items as oats; jam; jute; journalism; ships' engineers; doctors; James Boswell; shortcake biscuits; the populations of Canada and New Zealand; the Presbyterian religion; kilts; Burns Nicht (popular in Canada and New Zealand); Andrew Carnegie; golf; high tenors who sing of the River Clyde; hairy tweed with lumps in it; Angus bulls; marmalade; television programmes on New Year's Eve; Labour politicians with pale faces, forelocks and fierce convictions; white heather; swingeing literary criticism; smoked salmon; bits chipped off the Cairngorm Mountains and made into cuff-links; broth; putting the shot (a gentle game played by fat men all by themselves); shinty (an exceedingly rough game, a murderous form of hockey); curling (a game like bowls-on-ice played by sliding forward small anti-personnel mines with a handle); venison; oil; and even more whisky.

The geographical features need not detain us too long as they are there for all to see. Most of the geography of Scotland consists of mountains, grass, heather and Edinburgh. As there is a steady rainfall, particularly during the Edinburgh Festival, there are a number of lakes. As these are land-locked they have been given the Scottish name of 'lochs'. One of these, Loch Ness, has not got a monster in it but the locals are keeping the fact quiet. The word 'loch' is pronounced like the word 'lock' except that you clear your throat rather noisily at the end. There is a lot of throat-clearing when speaking Scottish words.

And so we come to the history of Scotland – about as well known to foreigners as the history of Fernando Po. Scotland is very ancient but little is heard of it before religion arrived. This is not surprising as only the religious could write things down. And, come to think of it, read what was written down. There must have been lots of lads dashing about the glens and washing their things in the burns and having bairns and so forth but what they got up to was not recorded and is beyond our ken ('beyond our ken' is a Scottish phrase meaning, roughly, not known to Kenneth McKellar – a high tenor who sings of the River Clyde).

Religion came to North Britain when a load of Irish monks sailed round the coast and tried to establish a monastery on the island of Lindisfarne, just south of Berwick-upon-Tweed (or, as the Romans called it, ·St Albans). The monastery was not a success. It just did not take. The Danes levelled it. It tried to keep going making wine, honey, cork table-mats, opening the kitchen gardens as an animal park, but it languished. When last heard of it was a pop group.

Meanwhile another batch of monks had landed in East Fife and founded the cathedral, town and university of St Andrews – arguably the most beautiful little town in the whole of Scotland.

Infant mortality was so high in those primitive days and so few people managed to survive into old age that the period is known to historians as the Middle Ages. During the Middle Ages religion and literacy spread out from St Andrews until the whole country was opened up to learning. This meant that records were kept and we now know what life was like in the remoter areas.

Life in the Highlands was always much grimmer than it was in the fertile Lowlands. The ancient Highland blessing of 'lang may yeer lum reek' is an indication of this, meaning 'long may your chimney smoke', that is to say, long may you be able to keep warm by having in your possession something to toss on the fire, like a faggot, or a Campbell. It is unwise to use this old expression when talking to a non-Scottish stranger as it sounds to untutored ears like an Old Testament curse to do with boils and private parts.

The Highlanders traditionally wore the kilt. There is some interest as to what a Highlander wore below his kilt. The answer is simple: below his kilt a self-respecting Highlander wore – and still wears – shoes and socks.

Over their shoulders the Highlanders wore a rolled up piece of woollen cloth which they called a 'plaid'. At night, up the mountains, when the snow lay on the heather and the air was below freezing point, the Highlander would find a 'burn' (a small poetic stream), dip his plaid into the icy water, wring it out and then roll himself up in it to keep warm. This practice produced men so tough that they formed the nucleus of what is now the famous Coldstream Guards.

This hardiness was expressed annually in the Highland Games, a series of contests in which beefy Scotsmen, clad in vests and the kilt, blood-lust aroused by skirling bagpipes, competed against one another in front of royalty and American tourists. The height of the Highland Games was reached when they were mounted in front of Queen Victoria and her entire Cabinet. A new item was introduced to mark the occasion, 'throwing the hammer'. In this the participating Scotsmen picked up a fourteen-pound weight on the end of a length of chain, whirled it round and round, gathering momentum, and then launched it in the air, the object being to drop it on the head of the Englishman who was Secretary of State for Scotland.

Perhaps the greatest contribution which Scotland has made to international affairs has been to develop the game of golf. This takes us back to the beautiful little grey stone fishing town of St Andrews, for its links – the Old Course – is the home of golf. It is there that the rules were formulated: that the game should be scored like a man waiting to be sentenced for a crime, or waiting for news of a wife having given multiple birth – the lower the number the better. That any player whose ball hits a seagull shall be said to have scored a 'birdie'. Or, if the bird is much vaster and rarer, an 'eagle'. That the ball shall be dimpled like a bishop's knees. That the hired assistant who prepares the 'tee' should be called a 'caddy'. Recognition of the St Andrews Golf Club's enormous contribution to the game came when, during the last years of the frail Queen Victoria's life, the name of the club was changed in her honour to the 'Royal and Ancient'.

St Andrews has many claims to fame, of course – the discovery of a sea salt in local seaweed which proved to have a beneficial effect on the liver and became famous as 'St Andrews Liver Salts', the extraordinary way in which students always seem to elect as their Rector men of enormous wit, charm and modesty. But to the ordinary visitor to Scotland St Andrews is not only the cradle of Scottish culture but also, perhaps more importantly, its most beautiful town.

This claim does not go uncontested. Many people claim that other coastal towns in East Fife and further north are even prettier. Arbroath, for instance, where the 'smokies' (small fish cured over smouldering fag-ends) come from.

I cannot agree.

The fact is that St Andrews, once the head of religion in Scotland, escaped the various evangelical movements of the last century, whereas almost every street corner in Arbroath has a 'kirk' built on it; a Wee Free, or a Seventh-Day Evangelist Mission, or a Presbyterian.

To my mind there is no doubt that St Andrews wins the contest for Scotland's most beautiful town, if only for one fact:

Too many kirks spoil Arbroath.

Book of Isaiah, xiv:ii

IF I were asked to enumerate the Seven
Deadly Virtues, the one I'd put right at the top of my list –
even above A Sense of Humour and Speaking Frankly – is
Female Tidiness. It is my belief that a houseproud wife can
undermine the male ego infinitely more destructively than
can any so-called 'liberated' housewife. In my opinion –
which I respect – it is not the orgasm-seekers who have
made contemporary men insecure about their masculinity,
it's the cushion-plumpers and picture-straighteners.

The most heartbreaking proof of that I can offer you is
the case of Dolly and Gerald. (As is customary when citing
case-histories, I am only identifying them by their Christian names because to reveal their surnames would be
grossly unethical.) (I am opening this additional bracket
just in case when you saw those Christian names your first
thought was, 'I bet I know the couple he's talking about;
they're the Dolly and Gerald who live in that road just past
the traffic-lights, he drives a Lancia, she's got her own
pasta-maker.' Because they are not *that* Dolly and Gerald,
honestly they're not. Word of honour.) (Don't go mentioning what you just thought, though.)

In many respects, Dolly was an ideal wife – attractive,
caring, intelligent, stinking rich – but in matters relating to
keeping her home neat and tidy her finickiness reached the
height of fanaticism. There can't be another woman in
north-west London who sets aside an hour every Friday
afternoon for boiling wire coat-hangers. And that was only
one symptom of an obsessiveness you could discern the

moment you entered their house. 'Gleaming' didn't do justice to what met your eyes. The floor of their front hall was polished to such a high degree of gloss, it was like coming into a bowling lane.

'It helps preserve the parquet,' Dolly would explain – and, to be fair, I suppose it sometimes did. So smoothly had that hall floor been waxed, I've seen an unwary visitor enter the front door, take one step forward, and the next time he stopped he was in the back garden.

There were many other respects in which spending an evening with Dolly and Gerald became Urban Stress at its most exquisite. 'Try not to leave footprints on the carpet,' she'd trill from upstairs while you wandered about the front room looking for somewhere to sit. This search was made necessary because all her armchairs and sofas were encased in slipcovers of protective transparent plastic. These are not only peculiarly unwelcoming – it's like sitting on a shower-curtain – but, in an odd way, slightly eerie. (If you spill a drink on one, it *stays* there.)

There was never any point in trying to relieve one's tension by lighting a furtive cigarette because where these were concerned, Dolly's early warning system was remarkable. One sniff of smoke and in she'd charge like Cochise leading a war-party. 'What are you doing with your ash?'

'I'm thinking of swallowing it,' I once said, hoping the implied rebuke might disconcert her.

Fat chance. 'You know we have a special room for anyone who wants to smoke,' was her smiling reply as she led me out to the toolshed.

Eating in that house was another aspect of her hospitality which demanded nerves of steel. By consequence of such unavoidable dining-table hazards as crumbs, soup-spill or spongecake splatter, it was impossible not to be made aware that Dolly would far rather have fed us all intravenously. As it was, not only did we have to endure her refusal to serve any plate of spaghetti until she'd taken a fork and combed each strand into a mathematically straight line, but her recipes for any kind of dessert always included the addition of a pinch of detergent powder. 'It puts such a gleam on the plates when I wash them up,' she'd murmur dreamily.

Of course, the one all our hearts went out to was Gerald. It is difficult enough to withhold compassion from a man who has elected to spend his life with a woman who polishes ice-cubes, but the more we found out about his domestic circumstances, the harder it became to remain unmoved. Imagine a wife who not only insists that her husband parks his car so that the name on the hubcap is always exactly parallel with the kerb, she also makes him put away all his clothing in strict alphabetical order. (Have you the remotest idea how much it costs to have a wardrobe that's fitted with twenty-six drawers?)

Opinions differ as to exactly what it was that finally drove Gerald to do what he did. Some say his breaking-point was reached when she hoovered his stamp-collection; others claim it was after she'd had him standing for two hours trying to straighten a watercolour of the Leaning Tower of Pisa. All we know for certain is that one morning Dolly came into their living room to find him hanging from a ceiling-fitting. (I dismiss as malicious gossip the rumour that her immediate reaction was to moan, 'Oh, Gerald – you'd look so much better in the other corner.')

Although it could be said that Gerald's final act did, in some way, redeem his dignity – they found a will stipulating that he be cremated and his ashes scattered all over her best dining-room rug – I still think there's a place in those books about Feminine Ailments for a condition called Terminal Neatness.

There is, I repeat, a lot of it about – and anyone belonging to the male sex must be alert to the syndrome. Should any female betray her feelings for you by such typical early symptoms as 'straightening the tie', or 'flicking a speck off the lapel', then my advice is – repel her advances immediately!

Or, to make use of Isaiah's succinct warning–

'Watch, men – ward off the neat!'

Shall I compare thee to a summer's day?

William Shakespeare

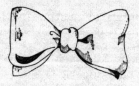

LITTLE in history turns out to be quite what we were told at school. Keats wrote in his 'On First Looking Into Chapman's Homer' that the stout explorer and conqueror Cortez stood 'silent, upon a peak in Darien'. We now know that at the time he was, in fact, putting Mexico to the sword and, far from being silent upon a peak, was being very noisy in Chihuahua. The lad who stared at the Pacific and who exchanged glances of wild surmise with his fellow sailors was another explorer entirely, a slightly furtive, thinner explorer called Bilbao.

One is left with the impression that most of history is an exercise in sleight-of-hand; or, in the case of the wrong explorer standing in the right place, sleight-of-foot.

One after another the old beliefs are shattered. 'Purcell's Trumpet Voluntary' – you know, 'Dadiddleiddleiddle-iddleiddleiddle-Da-Di-Da-Da-*Dah*-di-da-didi-da-da' – was not written by Purcell but by another composer, Jeremiah Clarke. The screen tough-guy John Wayne's real name was not John but Marion. Dick Turpin was a small-time, violent crook who did not ride to York (somebody else did but I forget his name). 'Birdseye Peas' are not so called because the word 'birdseye' conjures up visions of something small, bright and wholesome but because the principle of deep-freezing was developed by an American explorer named Clarence Birdseye (explorers seem to get everywhere). Mrs Beeton did not write, 'First catch your hare'. Students are referred to the eighteenth-century writer on cookery, Hannah Glasse. She did not write it either.

And now another myth is exposed.

I am able to reveal that Shakespeare did not write the opening line of one of the loveliest of his romantic sonnets, i.e. 'Shall I compare thee to a summer's day?' It was written by Bacon.

It is important to explain at this juncture that the Bacon in question was not Francis Bacon, the essayist and statesman, but T. Harcourt Bacon, an actor in Shakespeare's company.

Throughout the history of drama it has been the misfortune of almost every company of actors to have a colleague such as T. Harcourt Bacon in their midst. That is to say, a decrepit old bore who had been with the company too long to be got rid of easily and who was almost uncastable as an actor.

Shakespeare's particular cross-to-bear was not only ancient but was incapable of remembering lines and those few which he did remember were delivered in a deep, resonant, incomprehensible mumble.

He was also a religious maniac, being a member of an eccentric sect known as the Eighth-Day Brethren of the Pentecost (Southwark Chapel) who made their point every alternate Friday afternoon by stripping naked and running through the City of London with a brazier of live coals on their heads calling 'Repent or Burn!' Most of them did both before getting back to base. These sorties earned T. Harcourt Bacon the nickname of 'Streaky'.

It was a damp Friday afternoon in a backroom of the Boar's Head tavern, the meeting place of actors and poets, on 23 October 1608. Shakespeare sat at a table by the window, quill in hand, trying to think of something to write about. In truth he was a bit short of money for the furnishing of New Place, Stratford. The trouble was that plays brought him prestige but not much cash and there were chairs to buy, candles, a second-best bed . . . the list seemed endless. Shakespeare finished nibbling his quill, spat out the feathers and sharpened up another, ready for inspiration.

'Masques!' Ben Jonson had said. 'The king loves 'em! Hardly any dialogue. Just write "Enter eight ladies-in-waiting from the ceiling on swans" and Inigo Jones does the rest. It's a doddle!'

'What are the fees like?' Shakespeare had asked.

'Dunno,' Ben Jonson had answered. 'All I've received so far from the king is a terce of canary.'

'What sort of canary is a tersoff? Does it sing?'

'No. Canary *wine*. A terce is a barrel.'

'How much does it hold?'

'Dunno. It's in the new Continental measure.'

But Shakespeare did not reckon that there was a future for him in masques. No, the new thing was books. Write a book of poetry. Dedicate it to somebody important who would take an interest in it. Get it published and sit back and count the takings. That was where the steady money lay.

Shakespeare had already worked out to whom he was going to dedicate his book. In those days books were printed, published and sold from the printer's shop. A few were sold at a discount to booksellers and pedlars but there was no system of distributing them widely. Then a bright young man, seeing that passengers on stage-coaches needed reading material, decided to open up booths at coaching inns. The bright young man was named W. H. Smith. Soon every coaching inn in the country had a little stall close to where the passengers embarked which sold books, journals, nuts, etc. and each had Mr Smith's name above it. Shakespeare decided to flatter Mr Smith and thereby get his book sold throughout the land. He had already composed the dedication.

It read 'To the onlie begetter of these ensuing sonnets, Mr W.H.'.

All he had to do now was write the sonnets themselves, but it was not proving easy. First of all he had been interrupted by Streaky Bacon stripping off for his Friday afternoon trot through Eastcheap and then failing to light his brazier. Shakespeare had to stand on a chair and try to light the coal with a candle but the hot wax kept dropping on Streaky's bare flesh. And then there was trouble with his actors who were rehearsing for their autumn provincial tour.

Each autumn the company went on tour with a revue. This consisted of funny bits from the plays and scenes set to music, for instance the Portia scene in *Merchant of Venice* where the cast went into a dance and sang 'A-tisket, a-tasket, don't choose the golden casket'. All very lighthearted. The revue was compèred by Dai Llewellyn, a comedian who took Welsh parts and did a nimble hornpipe as well. Unhappily Dai Llewellyn had more theatrical sense than he had common sense and the night before, at a performance in front of Queen Elizabeth, he had done an impression of Sir Walter Raleigh, who was in the Tower for treason, which had so upset the Queen that Llewellyn was sent to join him. So the tour was due to take to the road the following day without a compère.

Just as Shakespeare was finishing eating his fourth quill, the door opened and Streaky Bacon staggered in, soaking wet, with his brazier hissing and making smoke.

'You look put out,' said Shakespeare, always a great believer in a little comic relief.

'Too bloody wet for saving souls,' mumbled the evangelist, wrapping himself in the curtain and drying himself vigorously. 'Laddie –' he began cautiously. 'I think that I should go on tour with the rest of the thespians. My experience will be of great use and I am up on the words of all the major roles, Richard the whatsisname, Henry the thingummy, that fellow with the gut . . .'

'Falstaff?'

'Who?'

'Sorry, Streaky, all the parts have been allocated.'

'Ah. Shall I superintend the lighting, my dear fellow?'

'We haven't got any lights.'

Streaky towelled away for a minute in silence. Then:

'The excellent woman who keeps my lodging-house is being a mite awkward about the rent. And I owe the coal-merchant a fair bit for brazier fodder. Shall I stage-manage the trip?'

'Sorry, Streaky. Burbage has put in his brother-in-law.'

'Young Llewellyn has blotted his copybook and there is nobody to introduce the items . . .'

'Streaky, *please*. I am trying to start a poem and I need peace.'

There was silence for quite a few minutes while both men struggled with their thoughts. Then, from Bacon:

'May I put a wee idea into your fertile head, laddie? You would do well to think on't.'

'Any idea would be better than this awful nothing.'

It was then that Streaky Bacon said:

'Shall I compère the tour, same as Dai?'

'I'll Gladly Go from Rags to Riches'

Richard Adler and Jerry Ross
Popular song

THIS is by way of being my Auto Biography; in other words, a chronicle of the hate–hate relationship which has blossomed between me and the second-hand dealers from whom I've bought the automobiles in my life. If your first reaction is to ask why I've never chosen to buy new cars, the answer to that lies in my firm belief that those feelings of anguished resentment which so quickly follow the purchase of any kind of car today are somehow less keenly experienced when the car is a second-hand one; possibly because the discovery that you've been gypped doesn't come as so much of a surprise.

In any case, there are two reasons why that lack of surprise is now more or less total. Firstly, I've learned that second-hand car dealers, like cats, can sense when someone is afraid of them. Secondly, since I'm what might be termed technologically retarded, by the time I've driven any car for longer than twelve months, it's in such a clapped-out condition that whatever substitute a dealer offers me in exchange can always be represented as an improvement.

As an example of that, let me take you through what happened on my last transaction. The car I'd been driving for the previous three years had developed disabilities of such magnitude that had it been a horse you would have been obliged to shoot it. Like the course of true love, it never had run smooth but by now the only part of it that didn't make a noise when in motion was the hooter. Even disregarding some of the minor frailties to which it had become subject – if you kicked a tyre, the wing-mirror fell off; whenever you turned the radio on, the windscreen wiper slowed down – something in the nature of a major defect had begun afflicting the braking system. You've read about those supertankers which have to travel ten miles before they can come to a halt? A similar tardiness of response was observable whenever I applied brake-pressure. If I wanted to pull up in Park Lane, I had to begin putting my foot on the pedal halfway down the Edgware Road. And even when I did manage to stop the vehicle within a stone's throw of its intended resting place, after I'd switched off the ignition the whole inside of the bonnet would go on shaking for about three minutes, like a dog coming out of water.

It was a motor which, as I was the first to acknowledge when I finally took it to a dealer for exchange, was not one he could honestly describe as being in showroom condition.

'What exactly is the matter with it?' he asked, fondling the dead carnation in his buttonhole.

'I think it's beginning to self-destruct,' I acknowledged. 'What can you show me?'

He cast a professional eye over the car's general appearance. 'Everything bar respect,' he said. 'But we'll find you something.' He drew my attention to a large American car which had what looked like a cousin of his asleep on the back seat. 'Fancy one of those? Lovely job.'

He switched on the engine, which coughed a little, then emitted an impressive vroom. 'Beautiful, isn't it. Only thing that'll pass you in this is a plane.'

'Why is white smoke coming up from it?' I ventured to ask.

He drew me closer. 'It was previously owned by a Pope.'

'I really had in mind something a little smaller.'

'Something smaller? Ah, now.' He took me over to a bright red saloon, lifted its bonnet and motioned me to look inside. 'Cast your eyes over this, squire. Who's a lucky boy then?'

As I've mentioned, when it comes to mechanical assemblies, anything more complex than a door-knocker and I'm banjaxed. However, not wishing to refuse his invitation in case it might confirm me as being even easier meat than he'd supposed, I bent low over the engine and, assuming what I hoped was an expression of eagle-eyed expertise, plucked at what looked to be an efficient metal bar. The bonnet fell down on my neck. Lifting it off me, he said, 'You've got a little beauty there, Sir Percy.'

'How many miles has it done?' I asked.

They never answer a question directly. He said, 'One owner. That's all it's had. Just one careful owner.'

'Have you got his name?' I asked.

'You wouldn't know him,' he assured me. 'A fellow called Herz.'

I hesitate to use the expression 'rip-off'. One does not wish to malign a whole profession when the majority of its members are probably every bit as transparently honest as they look. However, I am impelled to confess that my subsequent association with that bright red saloon has turned out to be just another Action Replay of the doomed affair between me and the internal combustion engine. We've been together now for eighteen months and the last time I took it for an MOT test, they warned me that the only parts of it which could be considered roadworthy were the sunvisor and one ashtray. Not only does it suffer from a condition that is technically known as 'oversteer' – in layman's terms, this means that if you blink hard while driving the whole car turns left – but it's so chronically underpowered that if I'm going past a schoolboy with a magnet in his pocket, I have to fight for control of the wheel.

Which means two things have now become inevitable. One, the car has reached the condition where I have to begin arrangements for exchanging it for another and two, whatever dealer I take it to will offer me an alternative which will simply set the whole sorry cycle in motion yet again. Without wishing to appear paranoid on the subject, I do get the distinct impression that, as far as the cars in my life are concerned, it was Tony Bennett who sang what is almost my theme song:

'I'll Sadly Go from Wrecks to Rip-offs.'

A source of innocent merriment

W. S. Gilbert
Line from 'I've Got a Little List'
'The Mikado'

E<small>ACH</small> year at about this time it is my practice to take a large foolscap notebook and a used bus ticket.
I enter into the former a list of my failures for the year and
on the back of the latter I note my achievements.

I very nearly filled the notebook this year. What sorry
reading it made. What a monument to the vanity of human
hopes: page 5, item 9, 'Try to entice cat down from apple
tree. Fall off ladder and break collar-bone (the small plastic
stiffener in my shirt-collar) which I then cannot get out of
its little tunnel. Try using pliers and tear collar right
across. Throw pliers on floor in exasperation. This disturbs
dog who wakes up in terror and is slightly, but tellingly,
sick'.

Or page 3, item 14, 'Decide to try jogging as an aid to
health. Soon break out in heavy sweat – hot on forehead,
cold on back of neck. Difficulty with what to do with arms,
which keep flying about like those of rag doll. Finally ram
hands into trouser pockets. Find this puts me off balance
and I keep banging into things with my shoulders. Left
ankle goes. No pain but ankle does not respond to instructions and foot dangles uselessly at end of it like broken golf
club. Hop on. Breathing becomes difficult and cannot see
clearly as red mist has descended over landscape. Heart
worrying as pounding so loudly that the noise might frighten
passing cars and induce accident. Decide that I will never
make it as far as the front gate so have a rest and walk back
up the drive'.

Or page 15, item 6, 'Collect wife's dress from cleaners as

going out that evening to dinner party. Am standing holding the dress over my arm when lorry passes v. close to me. Hook of wire coat-hanger catches in rope securing lorry's load of iron rods and dress is snatched out of my arms. As lorry disappears round bend with dress, note that it says on the backboard "Thos. Greenhough Ltd. The Ironworks. Huddersfield".'

Or page 38, item 12, 'After wife has been trying unsuccessfully for twenty minutes to start lawn mower, offer to do it for her by dint of superior strength, etc. Take firm hold of toggle and give a long mighty pull. Pull is longer than the cord. Cord snaps. Mower falls on to its side. Petrol and oil leak out killing grass. I, released from strain, hurtle backwards, trip over wheelbarrow and fall heavily, breaking comb in rear trouser-pocket and demolishing tiny dogwood tree just planted to commemorate thirty years of marital bliss'.

And so on. Perhaps the most poignant entries were on the last page, page 54, items 16 and 17: 'Once again note, with heavy heart, that the Nobel Prize for Literature has gone elsewhere. Nothing for yet another year from the judges, not even a book token'.

In marked contrast, I could not think of one thing to write on the back of the bus ticket. The only achievements that sprang to mind, after an hour's deep thought, were that I managed to cut my toe-nails without also cutting a toe, and I glimpsed Esther Rantzen in the Oxford Street Woolworths. Neither of these seemed to be achievements of a high enough calibre to merit being recorded so I tore up the bus ticket and sank into melancholy.

'Had it always been thus?' I mused, miserably. 'Have I never achieved *anything* memorable? Has not only this year been unfertile but the whole of my life?'

Then I remembered. I *had* achieved things when young. I had received prizes and awards. And, what is more, I had kept them.

There they were still. Up in the loft, between a dead deckchair and a hand-propelled sewing machine with angels all over it, in a cardboard suitcase marked 'F. Muir. Trophies. Do not disturb or a curse will fall upon you'. I dusted off the case, took it downstairs and, unmindful of the curse in my excitement, opened it up.

There they all were, lovingly wrapped in pre-war copies of the *East Kent Messenger*. The very first prize I ever won – a cup and saucer with 'God Bless the Prince of Wales' printed in large red letters. I have total recall of the occasion. Broadstairs sands. Uncle Mac's Minstrel Show Amateur Talent Contest (held every Wednesday morning to stiffen the takings). I was aged seven and decided that in spite of having no front teeth I would regale them with a song. There was a sensational film 'White Cargo' doing the rounds at that time which featured a torrid love affair between a tea-planter and a tempestuous jungle beauty named Tondelayo. I sang the theme song, which went 'Tell me, Tondelayo, wild jungle flower . . .' In the absence of any other competitors I was awarded first prize. This was so exciting that I fell off the platform and broke the cup.

I unwrapped another trophy. Yes, yes, the prize for selling most programmes for the Annual Water Sports! How I laboured. I used to run up and down the promenade pestering visitors, waving the programmes in their faces, until they bought one to get rid of me. On the day before the sports I skipped school and got a head start on the other programme sellers and won the prize, a quarter of a bottle of red stuff which said on the label 'Vino. Product of Italy'. My father said it was horse liniment and I was not to take it internally so I put it away.

A tiny little bottle came next, about the size of a third of a thermometer. Yes, of course, the scent I won at the first dance I ever went to! I sniffed it. It still gave off the unforgettable, heady fragrance of Phūl-Nana. Looking back, I rather think that it was a sample because it only held one drop which would not come out. I had to take the tiny stopper out and shove the bottle up my nose to get a good whiff. We had all been shuffling vaguely round the floor to the strains of 'Won't You Do, Do, Do What You Done, Done, Done Before, Baby' when there was a roll on the drums and Mr Potter said, 'Stay where you are, everybody! Now we come to the moment you have all been waiting for – the Spot Prize!' I won it easily, having at least half again as many spots as the boy who was runner-up (acne was disallowed).

The next item was much larger. A hand-mirror inscribed 'Mackeson's Milk Stout'. Who on earth . . .? Oh, yes! Vicar! Mr Dinwiddie, who pumped the organ, was getting a little old for it and when Mr Firth, the organist, decided to end his voluntary with a tremendous crescendo of sound so that his wife up the street would know the service was nearly over and put the greens on, Mr Dinwiddie had to pump so vigorously that he put his back out. And I volunteered to pump for the evening service and the vicar gave me the mirror as a gift for, as he expressed it, 'doing him a service'.

My last trophy was a Curiously Strong Peppermint (without a hole in the middle. This was before confectioners caught on that customers would happily buy a hole if it had a bit of mint round it). The headmaster had announced that he would give a gold sovereign to the first boy to score a century in the annual cricket match against our deadly rivals, Chatham House. The first ball bowled at me was wide so I took a mighty sweep at it. Unhappily the top strap of my pad had come undone. As I swung round, the pad drooped out at right angles and demolished my wicket. The Booby Prize for the match was a Curiously Strong Peppermint.

Five fine trophies of past glories! And there was I thinking I had achieved nothing in life!

I reconstituted my torn-up bus ticket with Sellotape and began writing.

'No achievements indeed,' I murmured to myself. 'On the contrary, I've got a little list!—'

> A saucer
> Vino
> Scent
> Mirror
> Mint.

Peter Piper picked a peck of pickled pepper

Proverb

QUITE the oddest item to arrive in my post of late was an envelope bearing the name of one of London's most expensive and exclusive hotels. All it contained was a cassette, on which a soft male voice, speaking in a tone of confidential servility, had recorded the following message:

You won't know me, Mr Norden, but after listening regularly to your programme I realize how badly you could do with an interesting story. Well, on account of me being a night porter at this place, I come into contact with all sorts of human dramas of every kind, so I have had ample experience of the tragic and heartbreaking events what get enacted within the confines of an opulent international hotel, especially as I also do a lot of looking through keyholes. And the tale I would like to enfold to you now is the strangest one whereof I was ever involved in.

It took place no more than a month ago in our Renaissance Penthouse, a suite of rooms so vast and luxurious it makes the Taj Mahal look like a hostel. Orders came that it was to be reserved for an elderly American millionaire of whom it had been learned that his Who's Who was twelve inches long. When he arrived on December 6th I found him to be an insignificant little old man, but that he was accustomed to having his whims obeyed became plain when he rammed me in the groin with a Bernini bronze for failing to draw the Persian lamb shower-curtains. Having thus chastised me, he then brought out a bunch of fivers the size of a cauliflower and behested me to purchase him the very finest pair of night-vision binoculars available.

It was only when I returned with these that he divulged me the bizarre purpose for which they were to be put to. Mr Norden, to say I was flabbergasted by it would be understating. So taken aback was I, I very nearly gave him the right change.

What it derived from was the fact that, although he was now rich beyond dreams of aviaries, his millions had only been acquired at the expense of the poor, the lowly, the under-privileged and the disadvantaged. In fact, that whole class of person obliged to buy at recommended retail prices. But now, in the twilight of his life, his conscience was smoting him. He wanted to make a gesture of recompense.

'Just one magnificent gesture,' he said. 'With these binoculars, I will spend the next few weeks looking down from this plush eyrie, scanning the shivering down-and-outs and tramps who are obliged to spend their nights on the Embankment benches below. Then, like some Caliph of old, I will select one single unfortunate, bring him up to this palace of opulence – and bestow upon him a night of such pleasures as he has never even imagined.'

My response was immediate. 'Why go to strangers?' I said. 'There's poor people all around.'

He gazed at me with contempt. 'Have you ever really known what it's like to be without in the midst of plenty?'

'Indeed I have,' I said. 'Wasn't I once caretaker in a girls' school?'

The backhander with the Bernini sent me clear into the bidet.

'I want a true pauper,' he said. 'The man my binoculars will be searching for must be starving, penniless, no home, no possessions, no hopes. And when they light on him, it is you who will pluck him from his degradation and bring him up here to the most unforgettable New Year's Eve of his squalid life. Not merely the finest food and wine money can buy, not merely the gift of marble bathrooms and satin bed-sheets – but also a night of almost unendurable ecstasy with the most desirable girl to be found in this great metropolis!'

I will freely confess to you, Mr Norden, that over the

next few weeks I was in a mood I can only describe as moody. The idea that all these benefits would go to some unwashed bum who probably wouldn't even appreciate them – it shuddered me even thinking about it. But every night the Caliph was there at the window, his binoculars peering down into the blackness in search of the last of the big-time losers. As the nights passed and no suitable candidate was found, my hopes rose a little. Perhaps he'd be unable to find anybody capable of living down to his expectations? Then, right at the very last moment – in fact, at seven o'clock on the night of December 31st itself – my hopes were shattered. Buzz went the indicator for the Renaissance Penthouse and when I got up there, the old boy was in a state of high excitement. 'Down there!' he said, pointing out the window and handing me the binoculars. 'The one curled up in the litter bin!'

I looked down and saw – well, how can I describe him? Filthy, unshaved, unkempt, ragged, bleary-eyed – and those were his more attractive aspects. 'Fetch him,' said Mr Millionaire. 'The rest is up to you. While I depart in my private plane for my private château on the Côte d'Azur in the Riviera of the South of France, conduct him hither and lay before him oysters, lobsters, pheasant, Charlotte Russe and the finest champagne in your cellars. Then, when a certain Miss McGinty arrives at five minutes past midnight, dim the lights, put on the Mantovani and withdraw.'

My heart sank. So it was to be Florence McGinty. Though the name is probably not known in the world you inhabit, Mr Norden, there isn't a red-blooded member of the free-spending, high-flying jet set who wouldn't pawn his Piaget for one hour with Cash Flo. Besides being one of the few girls who could get into the hotel lift and press the Up button just by breathing, she was someone for whom I'd harboured wriggling-about longings for so many years, I could now only moan and whimper.

But what could I do but obey instructions? Gritting my teeth, I collected the strong-smelling person from his disgraceful place of rest, conveyed him, blinking and muttering, to the silken splendours at the top of the hotel, set before him his unaccustomed and undeserved luxury fare, and departed.

It could have been the most disgruntling night of my life had it not been for a most unusual error on the part of Mr Ali Patel, our world-renowned French wine waiter. On his champagne order, instead of writing 'Four bottles of the '47', he'd put down 'Forty-seven bottles of the '4'.

The consequence was that when, at one minute past midnight, I made my accustomed round of the keyholes, what do I see through the aperture of the Renaissance Suite? There's Mr Unsavoury lying sprawled across the Charlotte Russe, dead to the wide. It was obvious what had happened. Because of the inordinate quantity of champers he had poured into a system grown unaccustomed to it – he and the old year had passed out together.

My mind raced. When the exquisite Florence came tapping at his door in less than five minutes time, about the only thing she could now expect in the way of fleshly delight was the Scottish Dancing belting out on BBC 2. Well, Mr Norden, if there's one thing in this world I hate, it's waste. So, in less time than it takes to tell, I'd opened that door with my master-key, bundled our friend down the laundry-chute, whipped-off my porter's jacket, slipped on a silk dressing-gown that had been supplied – and by the time that soft tap arrived, I was on the chaise longue in an attitude of negligent welcome.

Mr Norden, in expressing the doubt that you'll ever enjoy a New Year one-tenth as happy as mine, may I also hope that you can put this story to some good use. It occurs to me that the tale of how an eye-balling hotel servant appropriated a perquisite intended for an inebriated indigent might be covered by that old adagio:

'Peeping porter nicked a perk of pickled pauper.'

The better part of valour is discretion

William Shakespeare
Falstaff in 'King Henry IV, Part 1'

THIS is the love story of three girls. It is a sad story, particularly at the end if you can get that far.

The three girls went to boarding school together in the superior part of Surrey and they were inseparable friends. They all came from the same sort of background. They all lived in houses backing on to golf-courses and all boasted to friends who lived more simply, 'There are fairways at the bottom of our garden.' Their fathers were driven to the City in polished cars. The fathers never looked out of the windows but read balance-sheets in the back seat. At night they read with the help of a little light on an arm, and smoked a small cigar. The girls' mothers were all very thin from eating a lot of avocado salad and smoking a great number of low-tar cigarettes in a patent holder which was supposed to cure them of smoking.

All three girls were named after rich aunts in Great Expectation and their names were Leonora, Samantha and Deirdre. One evening, sitting in Deirdre's room, swapping Polaroids of their ponies, they swore a solemn swear that when they grew up they would all marry very rich men. They were eating a jar of caviare at the time which Samantha's mother had sent her as it was left over from the Golf-Club Fête's White-Elephant Stall. The three girls spread the rest of it on a chocolate digestive biscuit and each ate a piece to seal their vow.

The rest of the girls in the school were not at all surprised when they heard about the vow. Leonora, Samantha and Deirdre were so totally absorbed in the pursuit of luxury and the acquisition and disposal of pounds, shillings and pence that they were known to the school as L., S. and D.

Physically they were an ill-assorted trio and the general feeling in the Prefects' Room was that they had a one-in-three chance of marrying wealth. The one-in-three with the chance was D. (Deirdre) who even at that age was a great beauty and had a figure that would start the windmill turning on a Dutch landscape painting at forty paces.

S. (Samantha) was another matter. For one thing she was abominably thin. Rumour had it that when Miss Proctor (Geography and Personal Hygiene) first supervised the juniors' baths, she made S. clench a coat-hanger between her teeth when she pulled out the plug so that she would not be swept down the plughole. She also had much too much hair for a girl of that lack of width, and it hung dankly down, getting into everything.

L. (Leonora) on the other hand was vast and rectangular. She had shoulders like those of an American full-back and only tapered slightly down to unfortunate ankles. No bosom. No waist. When permitted to wear Own Clothes she favoured ankle-length black dresses. This, and the fact that her hair was a mop of frizzy beige, meant that from a distance she closely resembled a recently poured glass of Guinness.

After leaving school the girls were set up in a tiny, but suitably expensive, flat in a square in West Kensington and the parents began making vague plans for massive weddings for the three of them. Meanwhile the girls were installed by their fathers in approved jobs. D. was learning the Montessori Method of teaching kindergarten. L. had taken a Cordon Bleu course and was cooking directors' lunches, and S. was mucking out stables for a lightly-titled cousin of her Mummy.

Their problem was that they were not meeting eligible, i.e. rich, young men. L. and D. were certainly meeting very rich men in the course of their careers but L.'s men were old and heavily married and D.'s were between four and six years of age. S.'s clients were aristocratic enough but were horses.

So the three decided to take out their savings, pop their

pony brooches, sell their Hermes scarves and have a month's holiday at the most fashionable and chic hotel they could find in the Greek Islands. There they would hope, nay expect, to meet their Mr Right. Or rather, Prince Right. Or Sheikh Right. Or, better still, Lord Right of the Bank of England.

The weather was perfect. The sun bronzed them, they swam and played tennis and lay about in their bikinis. And all three fell deeply in love.

It was the Tuesday afternoon. S. and L., who had not won a single admiring glance from the rich young men in the hotel, went for a stroll along the beach and found that just round the corner was a group of chalets filled with a package tour of Britishers. No sooner had they sat on the sand when they were joined by two likely lads. Next to slim talkative S. sat vast silent Reg. Reg, it transpired, worked in a pet shop in Woking and loved all living things including, after three minutes, S. Next to vast bovine L. sat weasely wise-cracking Sid, a computer programmer from Slough. L. had never met anybody so wonderful in her life, so amusing and intelligent and worldly. She felt she could sit and listen to him for hours. Which is just what she did.

In a pink haze of happiness S. and L. floated back to their hotel as the sun began to sink. The first thing they saw was D. lying on the beach very close indeed to a bronzed figure. The girls shouted. The figure looked up, muttered something to D., waved and strolled away. He was young, dark, muscular and was very beautiful; a combination of Omar Sharif and Robert Redford, with a hint of Nureyev about the loins.

D. looked as though she had been hit on the head with a hammer.

Over dinner they came down to earth a little and exchanged stories. D. was absolutely appalled at what L. and S. had to tell. 'A shop-assistant! And an office clerk!' she screamed in her rather loud voice which sounded like a seagull with its foot caught. 'Oh, my dears, how *ghastly*!'

L. and S. stared at her in amazement. 'But Reg is *lovely*!' said S.

'Sid is *heaven*!' said L.

'But they are not *rich*!' screamed D. 'My Aristotle is

stinking rich! He is a nephew of Niarchos. Poor lamb has had *the* most *frightful* row with his uncle – something about a dozen supertankers his father gave him which uncle is trying to get off him – and he is lying low here for a few weeks. I shall comfort him, poor sweetie. Isn't he the absolutely, hyper most? Like a Grecian god!'

For the first time since they first met at school a rift grew between them. That evening L. and S. trotted down the beach for an Olde Tyme Dance at the chalet restaurant with their beloveds. They arrived back at their hotel at half past eleven. D. did not turn up at all. She staggered in at ten o'clock the following morn.

'He seems rather keen,' she said, and went to bed.

And that was the pattern for the rest of the holidays.

Aristotle, it appears, remained keen and L. and S. saw very little indeed of D.

When they got back to London they realized that their lives had changed irrevocably. S. took a job at a supermarket in Woking to be near her Reg. L. moved out too and became a waitress in Slough so that she could see her Sid at lunchtime as well as in the evenings. D. waited for her rich Greek to come and take her to her new life of unimaginable luxury. He had promised to collect her by helicopter as soon as the feud with his uncle was settled.

The three girls agreed to meet in London on the anniversary of their holiday and exchange news.

Which they did.

S. had inherited money from her aunt and she and Reg were going to open a stables and cattery in an animally bit of Sussex. They were getting married the following week. Sid, the computer programmer, had been promoted and was going to be the firm's Far East chief. He and L. were going to be married and were clearly going to do great things together on behalf of the company.

And beautiful D.? She spent most of her days looking up in the sky for the helicopter and bashing into lampposts.

The three old friends walked along the Edgware Road, looking vaguely for somewhere to eat and chatting away. D. was a bit ahead, eyes up to the sky, when they passed the Athens Kebab and Takeaway House. It was a hot day, the door was open and inside S. could make out two waiters in greasy vests. One was setting tables and the other was slapping butter into little pots and patting it flat.

'There's a restaurant!' said L. 'Kebabs, too. How suitable!'

'No!' said S. urgently. 'Quick – move on!'

'But, why?'

'See inside?'

'Yes. Just a couple of fellers working.'

'Look again . . .

'The butter-patter feller is D.'s Grecian.'

'Try a Little Tenderness'

Harry Woods/*James Campbell*/*Reg Connelly*
Popular song

IN an earlier episode of these readings, I happened to remark that the countryside bores me boneless. As far as I'm concerned, all it represents is an area where the trees may be more crowded but people are further apart. In fact, so incurably urban am I by temperament, were I forced to live within an unspoilt rural environment for any length of time, I am quite certain I'd wind up in one of those places where they take the laces out of your shoes. I can't help it, but prolonged exposure to clean country air leaves me in a state of such melancholy, they can only restore me to health by holding me near the exhaust of a bus.

It would be very difficult to exaggerate the storm of outrage which those off-hand remarks called forth from listeners. But I'll try. Perhaps the best exemplar was the letter that arrived from a Mrs O.W. of Surrey, because that one expressed hurt even in its form of address. Instead of starting 'Dear Denis', it began 'Poor Denis . . .'

'Poor, *poor* Denis,' it went on. 'If only you could be made aware of all the beauty you are depriving yourself of by this distrust you exhibit towards our most precious heritage. I pity you, poor Denis, I do really, I really pity you.' After continuing in this compassionate vein for a few more lines, it went on. 'May I make a suggestion to you, poor Denis? Soon it will be spring again, the time of year when Mother Nature calls to all her growing things, "Come on now – one more time." Denis, why don't you allow yourself to become *part* of that perennial miracle? Find some verdant pasture and, from the vantage point of a small tent, let yourself *experience* the lyrical marvel of earth's awakening. Do that but once, poor Denis, and I guarantee you that never more will you use the public airwaves to proclaim that all Nature means to you is the unseen force which lets birds know when you've just washed your car.'

Well, I'll admit it – Mrs O.W.'s letter got to me. I mean, somewhere deep inside. Although the argument sometimes expressed as 'If you've never tried it, don't knock it' is one that's advanced today in relation to everything from muesli to incest, it still has a certain force behind it. So much, in fact, that I resolved to take up the lady's suggestion. What follows, therefore, is by way of being a report to Mrs O.W., written in the first person rural, regarding my attempt at a reconciliation with natural phenomena.

Faithful to her instructions, on the very first weekend of spring – which arrived somewhere round the middle of July – I jumped in the car, betook myself to the nearest verdant pasture and struggled across it till I found a suitable site for pitching my small tent. I am glad to acknowledge, Mrs O.W., that even in that short journey I learned something about the countryside which I'd never realized before. Although I had often listened to that well-loved old spiritual 'Carry Me Back To Green, Green Pastures', it was only the experience of walking across one on which several cows had been grazing that taught me why its lyric insists so strongly on being *carried*.

My next lesson came when I was presented with the challenge of my tent. I have come round to the view, dear Mrs O.W., that you may have placed too much emphasis on its being a small one. As I measure some six-foot-three in length, I spent most of that night with everything below my knee-cap protruding from its entrance. Admittedly, this meant that the flap had to be left open, allowing me a different view of the night sky from the one I generally get between the chimney-tops – all those glittering stars stretching above like some huge connect-the-dots game – but whatever majestic thoughts that sight aroused in me were dispelled next morning when I awoke to find myself devoid of all sensation in my lower legs. I won't make too much of a sob-story of that because, on inspection, all it proved to be was the natural result of leaving them extended all night on damp grass; combined with certain after-effects from a cow sitting on them.

What I'll readily grant you, Mrs O.W., is that, to a born and bred city-dweller like myself, there really is something about waking up in a meadow. Not only are you conscious of a scent you've never encountered before – as though the whole world had been suddenly sprayed with Room Freshener – but there's nothing to beat that pure clean country air for improving the taste of your first cigarette.

In fact, as I stood by my small tent, drinking in all the rustic sights and sounds, I found myself thinking, 'This might yet turn out to be a really enjoyable weekend. Providing, of course, I can get out of this damn sleeping bag.' You see, Mrs O.W., owing to some difficulty with the zip, I'd woken up to find myself imprisoned within it. Apparently, it was a lady's model, and therefore fitted with some kind of chastity lock.

Sadly, even when I did finally succeed in cutting my way out of it, the day failed to brighten much because the floral pattern on my pyjamas attracted a swarm of bees, so that I had to return inside the tent till nearly midday. 'This is hardly getting up with the lark,' I remember musing when the swarm finally departed – presumably because it was now opening time for real flowers – but, determined to make the best of the time left to me, I slipped off my p.j.s and reached for my clothes. If I tell you it was only at that moment I noticed that some species of furry beetle had taken up residence inside my Y-fronts, perhaps you will understand why I was back in London just after one-thirty.

As you will appreciate from the foregoing, Mrs O.W. – I did try. But I think you'll have to live with the fact that there are some people for whom Nature just doesn't ackle. We are not all made the same, Mrs O.W. So what I suggest is that until such time as I can equip myself with a three-bedroom tent with underfloor heating and double garage, we cool it. You take the great outdoors and I'll stay with the grate, indoors. Once we agree on that, something I'd also advise is that next time you feel impelled to urge a certain unnatural course of action on a complete stranger, think for a little while first. I don't mean for long. Just, say, a decade.

And you'll know, of course, the unnatural course of action I'm referring to:

Try a little tent, Denis.

Messing about in boats

Kenneth Grahame
'The Wind in the Willows'

IT is a strange tale I tell. A tale of the bygone past. Of men and women long dead, of noble and of common birth both. There is danger in the tale, too. A very real danger of the whole thing becoming deadly boring before I have even started. So my story begins.

I happened upon my literary discovery quite by chance whilst browsing through the non-fiction section of Egham Public Library last Tuesday. Well, actually the Mobile Van which calls at our village on Tuesday afternoon. I did not mean to browse but Sonia does the non-fiction and as Mrs Spottiswode (Light Love, Crime and van-driver) is getting suspicious, I thought I had better pretend that I was in the van to pore over the books. With a hasty whisper to Sonia that I would meet her on Saturday morning at the super-market as usual between cat food and fruit yogurts, I picked up the first book to hand and buried my nose in it.

It turned out to be a very old book called *Curiosities of Literature* by the Rev. T. Thurlingwold Plackett (a name new to me). It was published in 1901 and in the front, in ink, was written 'To Captain Trumper – who kindly overcame my *idée fixe* that I could never love a man with a tattoo on his bottom – Lady Anne Plover, March 2nd (and a little bit of March 3rd), 1902'. I turned to the main text and was instantly enthralled. I was in for a few surprises, I can tell you.

Like me, you have probably always thought that national advertising first began in this country in the early years of the last century and that the world's first nationwide ads were for Warren's Blacking, Pear's Soap and Rowlands Macassar Oil. Not so, it seems. The first nationally advertised product was something very different.

Further. You have probably lived all your life under the delusion that Lord Byron was the first famous writer to write advertisements and that he wrote solely for Mrs Warren, of Warren's Blacking, who paid him £600 a year, a fortune in those days. You cling to the fact that the *Edinburgh Review* wrote: 'The praises of blacking were sung in strains which would have done no discredit to Childe Harold himself, even in his own opinion – for when accused of receiving £600 a year for his services to Mrs Warren – of being, in short, the actual personage alluded to in her famous boast, "We keeps a poet" – he showed no anxiety to repudiate the charge'. But I now know better. Three years before writing verse for Mrs Warren, Byron had written a fine piece of copy extolling the praises of a make of boot.

Wedging myself in the corner between Juvenile and Reference as Mrs Spottiswode took roundabouts at speed on the way back to Egham, and ignoring Sonia who was bent on nibbling my ear, I read on and on. What a story unfolded.

It all began one Tuesday morning in Wilton House, the Wiltshire home of the Earls of Pembroke, in the year 1583, when a son was born to Mrs Massinger, the wife of one of the family retainers. He was steward to either the fourth son of the second Earl or the second son of the fourth Earl – it was difficult to tell with all those winding staircases – and a trusted employee, so the little lad, whom the doting parents christened Philip, was allowed the run of the house.

Young Philip Massinger grew up to be a veal-faced lad, much given to solitary walks and book reading. He spent a great deal of time in his Lordship's library with his nose stuck in a book. This was an indication not only of the boy's love of literature but also of the fact that books were so strongly bound in those days that if your nose got in the way when you closed a book it was the devil's own job to wrench it free.

In the year 1603, when Philip was twenty years old, his parents died of a surfeit of Lampreys. Mr and Mrs Lamprey were deadly dull at the best of times and their coming to stay with the Massingers proved fatal to the old couple. The fourth Earl was most sympathetic to the young Philip, gave him five shillings (a miserable sum in those days) and sent him out into the world.

Within a year Philip Massinger had made his name as one of the brightest of the new wave of Jacobean playwrights. As the years passed his reputation grew. He wrote plays with the famed duo Beaumont and Fletcher; he became a friend of hit poet and playwright Ben Jonson; he married, had a son and, inspired, wrote the play he is best known by and which is still produced by the National Theatre when they want to bung on a cheap revival – *A New Way to Pay Old Debts*.

In 1640 Philip Massinger died. As far as the world was concerned that was the last that was to be heard of the Massinger family; the line disappeared without trace. Disappeared, that is, until the Rev. T. Thurlingwold Plackett started sniffing into the archives. The truth is stranger than fiction.

The old Earl took the Widow Massinger and her son back to Wilton House and let them live there. Now Wilton House is very, very old – parts of it go back as far as the A30 – and very, very large. The rooms he allotted the Widow Massinger were in the West Wing, which was in Hampshire, and the corridors were so long and winding that she never did manage to find her way out again. And so the Massinger son grew up within the maze-like confines of Wilton House. This was no hardship because a busy life went on back there. Gipsies arrived to sell clothes-pegs and could not find the exit. Burglars broke in and could not break out again. Curates arrived to solicit funds for repairing the organ and found themselves trapped for life. Young people fell in love, were married, started families. Life went on.

In the year 1781 the tenth Earl, a notable explorer, assembled a group of like-minded intrepid sportsmen and mounted an expedition into the interior of Wilton House. After three weeks of dangerous progress, bivouacking where they could, they reached the West Wing and discovered the tribe living there. The tenth Earl was particularly taken with young Thaddeus Massinger, an ingenious lad who was trying to make a water clock which ran on quarts of beer (it was history's first quarts timepiece).

Realizing that the boy had a future, the Earl had him wrapped in a stout sheet of brown paper and posted to London to be apprenticed to a bootmaker.

By 1790 Thaddeus owned his own bootmaking business in St James's and was on his way to becoming very rich indeed. (His subsequent career is beyond the scope of this work but it might be noted that he ended up a peer, Lord Last, and sole purveyor of unifoot boots to Queen Victoria's army. 'Unifoot' boots were army boots which fitted either the left or the right foot. Or, to be more accurate, did *not* fit either the left or the right foot.)

Thaddeus's success came from his brilliant inventions in footwear. Until he came upon the scene all footwear was either a shoe which buckled or a tall, loose, floppy boot. When farm workers walked through mud their loose boots stuck and they had to walk on in their socks. Thaddeus invented what he called 'gum boots'. The farm workers paraded in front of him and he poured a bucket of gum inside the boots. This stuck the boots on to the workers. For life. Not wholly satisfied with his gum boots, he turned his attention to light shoes and invented a white shoe which could be worn to play tennis in. It was made of canvas and soaked in whitewash. These proved so comfortable that the gentry took to wearing them as bedroom slippers. The trouble with them, though, was that they left trails of white powder on the landing carpet and next morning the hostess could tell from them where everybody had spent the night. They became known as 'sneakers'.

Thaddeus Massinger's breakthrough came with his invention of boots which did up at the side with buttons. For the first time in history the gentry could wear slim, close-fitting boots, tailored to their ankles. They swept through London society like wildfire until everybody who was anybody had a dozen pairs. And Thaddeus's sales fell off drastically.

It was then that he had his great idea, and the world's first national advertising campaign was born. Thaddeus decided to put an advertisement in every newspaper in the kingdom. He hired the great cartoonist Cruikshank to make an engraving showing an elegant pair of the boots, buttons prominently displayed. And he hired a noble but poor young poet, Lord Byron, to write the copy.

And this was what Byron wrote. At the top of the advertisement were the words 'There is nothing, absolutely nothing, quite so worthwhile as –' Then came Cruikshank's engraving. Then the world's first advertising phrase:

'Massinger Button Boots'.

'I Left My Heart in San Francisco'

Cross/Cory
Popular song

THANKS to a radio series called *My Music!*, it is now a matter of public knowledge that my singing voice is to melody roughly what bubble-gum is to gourmet cuisine. As the format of the programme requires each of its participants to perform a song every week, my constitutional inability to carry a tune, together with a certain nervous tendency to change key every fourth bar, have both become the subject of widespread comment, particularly from Frank Muir. Employing the privileged candour of an old friend, he frequently draws the attention of listening audiences to my vocal inadequacies with such telling phrases as 'sounds like a wounded moose recorded at the wrong speed'; or, 'I've experienced better harmonies from a leaking balloon'; or even once, in a spontaneously Shakespearian moment of eloquence:

> Oh what is so rare as a day in June?
> A song which Denis sings in tune.

It was therefore all the more surprising – I'm tempted to say touching – when I received a telephone call from him one afternoon suggesting I come along and sing a few songs of my own choice at a charity cabaret he was arranging that weekend. Even though I knew him to be one of the few people aware of the secret fantasy I've always nursed – namely, that some night, given the right conditions, my vocal shortcomings would miraculously disappear and I'd suddenly astonish an audience by displaying all the arts of a Sinatra or a Bennett – I still found myself deeply moved by his invitation. Controlling my emotions, I questioned him as to 'the venue of the gig' as we singers call it.

It was to take place in the grounds of his own home. He'd donated his spacious garden to a local charitable organization for a Saturday afternoon fête, which would be followed in the evening by a Disco to be held inside a large marquee on his paddock. Around 10 p.m. the dancing would be halted and Frank would announce an All Star Cabaret. Me. I would then go on and sing a selection of popular favourites, accompanied by the local church organist at the piano.

'But why me?' I couldn't help asking. It was a little ungracious, perhaps, but I was only too aware that Frank's wide circle of acquaintances included such luminaries of popular song as Jack Jones, Paul McCartney, even Vince Hill.

There was a pause. 'Because you're my friend,' he said gruffly.

Say what you like about this heartbreak world of show-business, I found myself thinking, but there are still nuggets of pure gold to be found among the dross. Without further ado I set about ordering a Lurex jacket and selecting my repertoire. After days of agonizing I came up with what was undeniably a shrewdly balanced programme. A driving up-tempo version of 'I Met Her on the Beach At Bali-Bali' to open, straight into a medley from *Gold-diggers Of 1929*, then – for my big crowd-pleasing finish – a really belting version of 'When It's Springtime in the Rockies'. As I said to Frank when I met him in the marquee that Saturday night, 'Something there to please all ages.'

His answering grunt seemed a little perfunctory, but it didn't disturb me. Discos aren't really my scene, either. What with all those flashing lights and whirling audio-visual effects, it's a bit like dancing inside a pin-table. Nor was I particularly worried when 10 p.m. came and went without that roll on the drums which is the prelude to a cabaret announcement.

However, when midnight arrived and there was still no sign of a halt in the frantic bopping, some slight agitation did begin setting in. Noticing that Frank was now boogey-ing with a neighbour who breeds Sealyhams – she's married to someone called Edward Sealyham – I approached him again. 'Excuse me, guv,' I said, 'shouldn't I go on and do my turn before the beer runs out?'

'Not yet,' he said. 'Not till it becomes necessary.' And with a whirl of his kaftan he was off back into the merry throng.

It was that word 'necessary' which sowed the seeds of suspicion. Noticing the church organist sprawled across the piano, I shook him awake and, while he was still bemused, put some questions to him.

Then it was that the whole sorry truth of the matter emerged. Apparently, after Frank had erected the marquee, he made application to the Council to approve its use as a place of dancing and entertainment. They'd sent along an inspector who looked round it, then shook his head regretfully. 'Sorry,' he said, 'I am afraid I can't allow this to be used as a disco.'

'Why not?'

'Fire regulations, Mr Muir. We can't have two hundred people crowding in here unless you can provide some means by which, if an emergency arises, you can get all of them out the place within twenty seconds.'

Whereupon Frank had pondered for a moment, then snapped his fingers. 'No problem,' he said. 'I know exactly how I can do that.'

'How?' said the Inspector.

'At the first sign of smoke, I'll get Denis Norden to *sing*.'

Do I need to describe my feelings on discovering such a betrayal? Without even stopping to think, I ran over to the group who'd been playing for the dancing, waved them to silence and requested a drum-roll. Then, before anyone could stop me, I stepped to the microphone. 'Ladies and gentlemen,' I called. 'It's Cabaret Time!' A hush fell over the audience. 'By arrangement with Frank Muir, we now present – SingalongaDen!' A nod to my accompanist and we were into 'Bali-Bali'.

Very seldom in a man's life does a futile gesture become a memory to treasure. But, without a word of a lie, my singing *paralysed* that audience. They were *spellbound*! Breathless with excitement and poor ventilation, they sat there and cheered my every song to the echo! Seventeen encores!

Mind you, it wasn't until the following day I learned that the people making up the audience were all beneficiaries of the charity for whom the evening had been organized; in other words, the National Association for the Hard of Hearing.

But even that knowledge doesn't diminish the thrill that flushes over me whenever I recall that performance. Nothing will ever erase the memory of the night when, against all odds—

I let my art entrance Frank's disco.

Many are called, but few are chosen

New Testament

SHOULD you ever have the pleasure of staying with my lady wife and me at our lovely home in Thorpe, Surrey (and you are more than welcome), you will sleep in what we are pleased to refer to as our 'New Testament Spare Bedroom'.

The reason we call it that might well be of interest to those of you of a scientific bent – or even those who are scientific but not bent – so here is the story, in all its strange and subtle beauty.

A while ago my wife and I watched a science programme on television. This was unusual for us as we are not in the habit of watching science programmes. In fact we are not in the habit of watching *any* type of programme. We believe that watching television is destroying the art of conversation so we ration ourselves to looking at one programme per year. We normally choose a programme which is concerned with something we are interested in, like the cheeses of Iceland or Arnold Bennett, but we happened to switch on when this science programme was in progress and we did not want to switch off in case we upset the man who was on the screen. It was one of those very serious investigative programmes in which young interviewers in dreadful little overcoats stopped people in the street and asked them things. And frightfully important scientists, looking like unemployed cellists, told us things in regional accents. And politicians, sleek and pale, kept saying 'Let us be quite clear about one thing . . .' and 'I have said before and I will say again . . .' and 'In a situation like the situation we are in . . .'

and 'As I said recently to the Home Seckertree . . .'

The burden of the programme, which came as something as a shock to my lady wife and me, was that very shortly, either in fifty years time or next Tuesday – the sound went wobbly and we are not certain which – all the oil in the world is going to dry up. One need not stress what repercussions this will have. The Arabs will have nothing valuable to sell to the West and will be reduced to penury and going round pubs with cardboard suitcases trying to flog sand to put into egg-timers. One will have to fry one's aubergines in dripping.

Worse than that, the programme pointed out, there will be no electricity. We will have no television once a year. We will have to drill little holes in our electric light bulbs and put nightlights in them. The pop-up toaster will remain cold and inert. Oil lamps which were expensively converted to electricity will have to be reconverted to oil and then, because there will not be any oil, thrown away.

But there is hope. It seems that we shall be all right – or all right for a week or two longer – if, instead of squandering our oil and coal and electricity, we eke it out. Chaps are now studying how best we can eke out absolutely everything – eke out trees, eke out food, eke out wildlife – in a new science which they called 'ekeology'. An ekeologist then came on the screen – he looked about fourteen, with staring eyes and hair like a Brillo pad – and told us to eke like mad; not to waste a drop of oil or a volt of electricity. Then there was a power cut and all the lights went out.

I swung into action immediately. I switched off the central heating thereby ekeing electricity and gas in one go.

Then came the problem of how to keep warm during the winter. It was not too bad during the day. We burned unekeable rubbish in the fireplace, like potato peelings and tea leaves, which gave off a bit of heat. Also the thick smoke which filled the house was not only acrid but also faintly warm. We developed a technique of dashing about the house all day at the double and eating our meals standing up and running-on-the-spot. The trouble came at night. The house is old, and winds creep in all over the place and find many cracks to creep out of, so in cold weather there is a constant icy gale blowing through the bedrooms.

I solved the problem of our own bedroom with beautiful simplicity. I bought a pair of baggy clown costumes from a theatrical costumier. When night fell and we retired (to save candles), we each donned our clown costume. These did up tightly at the ankles but were very loose about the body and had a wide neck. When my wife was safely within hers she stood still and I carefully poured buckets of sawdust down inside her collar and into her costume until she filled out and could accept no more. I then wedged rolled-up newspaper into her collar to prevent the sawdust escaping, sealed it with sticky tape and she was four feet wide but snug and warm. She then did the same to me and we rolled each other into bed.

My problem was the spare bedroom. I bought another pair of clown costumes but our guests did not take to them kindly. Nor were they all that efficient on some of our friends: the Bishop, for instance, who was so portly that the costume fitted him like a glove, leaving no room for sawdust to be poured in. It was a poser.

Then one day, musing on the theme of solar heating, I noticed my wife's greenhouse. Although cold in the garden, the interior of the greenhouse was snug and warm. And it was just large enough to take a double bed.

The next few days were busy ones. I began by buying a quantity of oak beams. These I installed in the dining room to prop up the ceiling, which was the floor of the spare bedroom and had to bear a great deal of extra weight.

Next task was to dismantle the greenhouse, number each part, cart it up to the spare bedroom and reconstitute it in the middle of the floor. There was a nasty moment when the double bed would not go through the greenhouse door. We overcame that by dismantling the greenhouse again and re-erecting it over the bed.

That night my wife and I slept in it to give it a trial run. It was not a success. We had left a quantity of vegetables still growing in the greenhouse and the night was so cold that we woke up frozen to the marrow.

It was my wife who spotted the design fault. The greenhouse was not getting any sun to warm it, now that it was in the bedroom.

I removed the tiles from the roof over the spare bedroom, hacked away the ceiling above the greenhouse and had the satisfaction of seeing sunshine – albeit thin and watery winter sun – pour on to the glass. I took the temperature inside at 4 p.m. and it stood at 84 degrees Fahrenheit. We had another trial run that night. Another disaster. At 4 a.m. the temperature had dropped to minus two and in the greenhouse it was cold enough to freeze the wheels off a Douglas DC3.

'But . . .' I said.

'Well,' said my wife. 'You see, when it was in the garden the sun warmed it during the day and at night a little electric heater came on.'

Pretty infuriating, you must admit. There was I, patriotically ekeing like fury, and all the time the potted plants were being kept happy on watts galore. I put my foot down, of course. No consumption of energy would take place in the spare bedroom of any sort whatwhomsoever. Somehow I had to think of a way of providing gentle, natural warmth within the greenhouse without using coal, wood, electricity, gas, oil . . .

In the garden next day I gave a great shout. 'D-U-N-G!!!'

'Is it one o'clock already?' said my wife, straightening up from her hoe.

'That was not the church clock striking,' I exclaimed, 'it was me! What is dung used to make? A – wait for it – a HOT-BED! If we fill the spare mattress with dung it will give off a constant natural heat, twenty-four hours a day! Quick, I will hold the mattress cover open while you fork the stuff in – Lady Muckberth!'

With a smile she got to work. We filled the mattress with dung, laid it on the bed in the greenhouse upstairs and in a moment it had begun giving off its gentle warmth. Nothing dramatic, of course, but the temperature never dropped below freezing point again.

'A good job jobbed, I think,' I said, putting an arm round my wife. 'Now all that remains is for you to cover a pair of clothes-pegs with padded cretonne for our guests' noses when in bed . . .'

Now, when we have guests to stay at our lovely home (and they are more than welcome), we can, without worry, put them to bed in our Old Testament Spare Bedroom. Many are cold, but few are frozen.

'The Stars and Stripes Forever'

J. P. Sousa

I don't know how you feel about going to parties in fancy dress, but as a source of pleasure I have always ranked it somewhere on a level with cleaning the oven. That's why, when I received an invitation last August from a certain rather florid magazine publisher inviting us to an opulent costume party to be held at his legendary country home, my overwhelming impulse was to weasel out. 'Make some plausible excuse,' I pleaded to my wife. 'I've been carried off by a UFO. The Welsh Nationalists are holding me hostage. I'm having labour pains. Think of *something*!'

She gave that sigh of patient tolerance with which those closest to me seem to greet so many of my most passionate utterances these days. 'I'm well aware how much you hate having to think up something you can go as,' she said. 'But this should be an easy one for you. The invitation asks guests to dress up as "The Title of One of Your Favourite Films", and you *love* films. So you should be able to think of *hundreds* you can design a costume for.'

Because my enthusiasm for indulging in any kind of dressing up cannot be understressed, I refused to rise even to that bait. Consequently, when we went to get the car out on the night of the party I was attired in my usual clothes. If reproached, I had decided to claim I was representing the title of a 1950s Gregory Peck vehicle, *The Man in the Grey Flannel Suit*. By contrast, however, my partner had really entered into the spirit of the thing. She'd found herself a fairly *dégagé* chiffon nightie, cut it even lower at the neck, and was going as *In the Heat of the Night*.

The trouble started when I suggested that an alternative title for her might be *Room at the Top*. She didn't take it very well. But it was when I went on to weave an engaging fantasy round the theme of *The Odd Couple* that her lips pursed to the size of a penny jam-tart. She jumped into the car and sped off into the night, leaving me alone in the garage.

It was apparent that I had gone too far. I also realized, from long experience of such moments, that the only chance I now had of restoring even a semblance of harmony would be to return to the house and penitently don something in the nature of real fancy dress.

It was at this point that I realized something else. Not only had she gone off with the car, but she'd also taken the house keys with her. In other words, whatever costume I might manage to dream up, it could only be assembled from the materials available in the garage.

A glance around showed these to be both few and unpromising. Hanging from a hook on a side wall were two old raincoats the kids used to wear for school. If I were to try climbing into those, could I get away with *The Blue Macs*? A moment's consideration and I rejected the idea, if only because it was never a film I could support as being among my favourites.

What else was to hand? (I silently cursed the uncharacteristic attack of neatness that had prompted me to clean out the garage the previous week.) Leaning against the back wall was an old perspex windscreen. Ah . . .! Suppose I cut a neat rectangle out of the seat of my trousers, then covered the hole with an oblong of the transparent perspex? Could I then pass myself off as the Hitchcock masterpiece, *Rear Window*? Or even, possibly, *Smiling Through*?

Neither possibility satisfied the complete transformation of dress I had to achieve if I were to be granted a parole from the doghouse. Then my eye lighted on something which fulfilled all the requirements – two chamois washleathers! By joining them together with the staple-gun they could be pressed into service as an unexceptionable facsimile of a jungle loin-cloth. It was the work of a moment to strip off, fasten the leathers around me, and there I was –

the undeniable title of one of my all-time favourite motion-pictures, *Tarzan of the Apes*.

I still believe my personal Jane would be talking to me today if the taxi I called to transport me to the party hadn't broken down half a mile from the publisher's country house. As it was, I was obliged to make the last section of the journey on foot and, not wishing to court undue attention by walking along the road in such an exiguous garment, I set off across the dark fields.

This, as has now been dinned into me, was my major mistake. I hadn't gone a hundred yards when there was a pounding of hooves behind me. Looking over my shoulder, I saw the most wicked looking bull I've ever set eyes on making towards me.

I don't know how many of you have ever tried running at speed in a tight leather loin-cloth? For those who haven't, let me explain that the faster you move, the tighter the loin-cloth constricts the area it covers. (In fact, I now take that to be the reason why the real Tarzan used to emit so many of those peculiarly high-pitched cries.) In the end, the garment became such an impediment that I realized the only way I'd keep ahead of the bull was to cast it off.

Which was why, when I finally burst through the hedge on to the lawn where the publisher's fashionable gathering was assembled, I was panting, sweating and stark naked. They, of course, took my nudity to be the costume I'd chosen to arrive in and immediately began exchanging guesses as to which film I was representing.

Some of those guesses were, I will admit, quite flattering. I was as taken by one gentleman's venture at *Splendour in the Grass* as I was by a certain lady's *The Greatest Show on Earth*. Other speculations, though, were as ill-mannered as they were inapposite. While I was somewhat affronted by my host's stab at *The Incredible Shrinking Man* the suggestion I really took exception to came from his daughter who, after one brief glance, proposed a film I didn't even think she looked old enough to remember: *Wee Willie Winkie*.

But it was a keen-eyed local farmer who brought me to the depths of humiliation. To justify his confident declaration that the only possible film title for me had to be *Midnight Cowboy*, he proceeded to point out that the animal from which I'd been fleeing hadn't actually been a bull at all.

It was that explanation which prompted the caption the local newspaper printed under a quarter-page picture their enterprising photographer had managed to snap of me while I was running across the field. Taken just at the moment when I was divesting myself of my loin-cloth in an attempt to escape from what could now clearly be seen as a young cow, it bore the words:

'This Tarzan strips for heifer'.

'Pickwick Papers'

Charles Dickens
Title of novel

I give you – and I am in no hurry to have it back – the Muir Method of Throwing a Successful Party.

One has only to think of famous hosts and hostesses of the past – the names of Signora Borgia, Count Dracula, Lady Macbeth spring instantly to mind – to realize that the failure rate of parties has always been high. In our modern world it has never been higher and it is, in my view, due to a basic misconception of what constitutes a good party.

The golden rule is simple and obvious but so important that every hostess should have it tattooed on her thigh – *people do not go to parties to enjoy themselves.*

People accept invitations to parties for a variety of reasons but the prospect of having a good time is seldom one of them. My researches indicate that 81 per cent accept because they are the victims of a mild form of moral blackmail and will lose face if they refuse. Eight per cent accept because they fail to read the invitation properly and think it is for something else. Six per cent do not know that they *have* accepted because their spouse has accepted for them. Four per cent accept because there is only a play about dying and a Party Political Broadcast on television. And 1 per cent have no choice.

The 1 per cent I met who had no choice was a lecturer in philosophy and linguistics at an emergent university on the east coast. Rigid with boredom, he had given up picking bits of the flock wallpaper off with his thumbnail and had begun hitting the wine-cup. I got to him just as his forehead went shiny and walked him round the block.

'What a boring party,' he mumbled to the stars. '*Boringly* boring, to boot. And boring *with* it . . .'

'Then why did you accept the invitation?' I asked, notebook at the ready.

'Had to,' he mumbled. 'I'm the wassisname . . . the host.'

Once you accept that none of your guests are there to enjoy themselves the whole philosophy falls into place. Clearly to give them an enjoyable time would be letting them down. They would forget the whole thing in an hour. But give them a subtly awful party and they will be able to pick it over and wallow in it in retrospect for months. A grievance shared is a grievance doubled. Your aim must be to send them home happily grumbling about all aspects of the evening.

To achieve this success needs careful planning and vigilant attention to detail. Nothing must be left to chance if everything is to go with a thud.

Guests can help a little in making the party fail to go with a swing. Quite a good idea is to grip your host by the hand when he opens the door to you and embark upon an immensely obscure and lengthy anecdote. If your timing is good you should be able to pile up other arriving guests behind you until a sizeable queue is waiting and grumbling. Making guests bellow with laughter when their mouths are stuffed with flaky *vol-au-vent* is an effective ploy, as is pressing a cup of coffee on a guest when she is already clutching a drink and her handbag in one hand and a plate of cheese and half a metre of French bread in the other.

But making a party ghastly/successful is mostly the responsibility of the hostess. She must be always alert for pockets of resistance, e.g. couples who are enjoying talking to each other (disgracefully antisocial behaviour). She must move instantly, take one of the malefactors firmly by the elbow and cry shrilly, 'I'm going to break you two things up! There's someone here absolutely *dying* to meet you . . .!'

Happy laughter anywhere in the room, unless it has an edge of hysteria to it, is a bad sign. An experienced hostess immediately bangs on the table for attention and screams, 'Food everybody!'

The food and drink which you serve are a vital element in making your party the most talked-about of the year. A successfully awful party is one where the hostess has clearly gone to immense trouble to provide fine, interesting food and drink and has, even more clearly, failed miserably.

The wine should be red (cheap red wine is much fouler than cheap white wine). As poor wine improves enormously on being served slightly warm you should serve yours straight from the fridge. It is important that the wine should not be instantly detectable as rubbish. The guests must be able to retain a slight doubt as to whether it is the wine which is at fault or their palates, so choose one of those extremely cheap plonks which have a homely label with a simple, seemingly honest inscription which just says 'Sound French Table Wine' or, even better, 'Red'.

Always have plenty of pretty bowls around filled with elderly potato crisps. Open the packets a few days before the party and give the crisps a good airing. They are ready when they look and taste like autumn leaves. Olives are always popular but make sure that they are not the stuffed variety but those which consist of a stone covered with immovable green skin. An optional extra is to provide oriental rice crackers. These are spotty little biscuits so hard that you will hear your guests' fillings crack like small-arms fire. They are very expensive, taste like earth and, before they had the bright idea of exporting them, were what Japanese peasants ate when they could not afford food.

For the more ambitious hostess, here is a list of prepared dishes. Next to the recipe I have given a name; this is in case one of your guests is drunk enough, or fawning enough, to exclaim 'This is delicious! – do tell me what it is!'

(1) Fine slices of brown plastic which stay in the mouth undiminished even after five long hours of chewing. PARMA HAM

(2) A bowl of shaving cream from an aerosol sprinkled with grated cheese rind. GARLIC WHIP

(3) Half a pint of white impact glue warming over a nightlight. SWISS FONDUE

(4) Small squares of old toast smeared with bacon rind, cleansing cream, dripping, sardine tails or anything. CANAPÉS

(5) Thin slices of stale Hovis spread with butter into

which a drop of cochineal has been dropped to make it pink, rolled up and rubbed on a kipper.

SMOKED SALMON FINGERS

(6) A failed omelet into which bits of ham have been thumbed, served on a piece of cardboard. QUICHE

My wife and I have operated the Muir Method of Throwing a Successful Party for some years now with only one failure that I can remember. It was a Burns Night Party and it went so well, according to plan, that after twenty minutes guests were looking at their watches and stifling yawns.

My big mistake was piping in the haggis. The haggis itself was perfect – my wife had made a shepherds pie, with porridge instead of meat, and stuffed an old football bladder with it – but I had misguidedly engaged four members of the London-Scottish Rugby Club to play the bagpipes. I put the steaming haggis on a silver tray and carried it from the kitchen out into the corridor to lead the pipers into the dining room. What a shock when I saw the pipers. They were all about nine feet tall and built like brick oast-houses. Below their kilts their calf muscles stuck out like watermelons. We formed up. I opened the dining-room door and marched in. Behind me four right arms clamped down on their bagpipe bags like legs of mutton clamping on grapes, and they blew. And there came forth noise.

Several things then happened at once. The Afghan hound rose in the air as if by levitation, hung for a moment on the curtain-rail and then pulled the whole thing out of the wall. They raised Tower Bridge. Two lady guests had hysterics and disappeared backwards over the rear of the sofa. The mirror cracked in two. The fire brigade arrived.

It was three in the morning before the last guest departed, wringing our hands and saying how much he had enjoyed himself – the whole evening was a total disaster. They had had *fun*.

Do by all means use the Muir Method for your next party but make sure that you do not make that one mistake that we made. If you have a Burns Night Party, pipe in the haggis – but, in the words of Charles Dickens–

Pick weak pipers.